I0510914

# THE PROHIBITED PERSONNEL PRACTICE OF THE INTERNAL REVENUE SERVICE

*J. Kligman*

© 2018 J. Kligman
All rights reserved.

ISBN: 1548430498
ISBN 13: 9781548430498

# INTERNAL REVENUE SERVICE UNLAWFUL NONHIRING PRACTICE, AN EXPOSÉ OF THE HOAX OF THE "RULE OF THREE" AS REASON FOR NONHIRING

The Internal Revenue Service (IRS) practices two methods of employment, one lawful, the other deceptive, unlawful, abetted by a judge of the federal district court.

This writing describes in detail both the IRS's unlawful practice and the deceptive handling of this case by a federal district court judge who hides her deception from public view.

Exposing unlawful IRS employment practice benefits attorneys in the practice of employment law, the applicants they represent, and alerts the public to the violations of law by the IRS that rules over the public, therefore a menace to the public.

# EXPOSED

Unlawful Personnel Practice of the Internal Revenue Service
Abetted by a Judge of the Federal District Court
Their Hidden Activity Revealed
a Case History

# TABLE OF CONTENTS

# INTRODUCTION

<u>Exposure of unlawful personnel practice of the Internal Revenue Service</u>

The purpose of this writing is to expose Internal Revenue Service (IRS) violation of employment law. The IRS has two employment practices, one lawful the other unlawful. Exposed is the unlawful practice, i.e., the stealthy, immediate dropping an applicant from the employment process absent "proper and adequate reason." Applicant is dropped when he states derogatory information in his application, convenient, "efficient," but unlawful IRS practice. Efficiency leads to salary increase. For IRS employees, salary increase overrides lawful practice.

This writing is also a primer for applicants and attorneys confronted with the law-violating personnel practice of the IRS. The practice is deceptive, disguised with the phraseology of law. The IRS, a powerful federal agency that violates law--while it rules over the public--is a danger to the security of the public.

<u>IRS's "failure to act" on the application for employment violates law</u>

The deception begins with the Selecting Officer, the individual who selects applicants for employment. I stated a conviction of mail fraud in my application. The Selecting Officer notes "conviction" and fails to act as though the application were nonexistent, a fraudulent "nonprocedure." The "failure to act," that is, the immediate dropping of applicant from the selection process violates law.

"Failure to act" is a legal "cause of action" against IRS in federal court. I do not claim an applicant with a conviction need be selected. I claim a nonselection must be lawful, i.e., "for proper and adequate reason." The "failure to act" is IRS unlawful omission of the reason for nonhiring. Queried for the reason, IRS employees respond with a chain of lies, including perjury, without fear of penalty.

## Significance of this case: IRS violation of law with impunity

The Selecting Officer's "failure to act," i.e., the immediate, unlawful but "efficient" removal of an applicant who stated a former conviction may seem trivial, a minor deviation of lawful procedure. However, IRS employees with the power to prosecute--while they violate law with impunity!--is not a trivial matter, but something to be feared. A law-violating IRS is therefore the significant aspect of this case. With the arrogance of power, IRS employees, believing themselves above the law, do not hesitate to violate law if perceived in their self-interest, such as gaining efficiency which leads to salary increase. Violation of law without fear of penalty reveals the IRS's stealthy, corrupt employment practice as normative.

Also significant is the trickery of a judge of the federal district court (Court), Mary A. McLaughlin, who, for personal convenience, refuses to review a "lawful cause of action," i.e., my complaint. She evades review with the pretext that the subject matter jurisdiction for review assigned her Court by the United States Constitution (Article III, Section Two), by statute, and by precedent does not exist. She dismissed the case, stating "issue preclusion" as ground, but in fact dismissed for lack of jurisdiction, a fraudulent change of ground, therefore a fraudulent dismissal. Evading review, she acts as "adjunct counsel for the defense," arguing on behalf of the IRS, defending the IRS in violation of judicial ethics. It is appalling that IRS employees and a district court judge violate oath of office and law in self-interest of convenience and, particularly for the IRS, "efficiency."

IRS employees defraud an applicant of the lawful right to compete for employment. A judge who argues on their behalf must, by necessity, argue deceptively and hide the deception. Accordingly, Judge McLaughlin labels the case "nonprecedential," does not publish it, thereby hides it, a travesty of lawful judicial procedure. A case unpublished, hidden, is a virtual admission of deceptive judicial practice.

### "Three considerations," the IRS's deceptive reason for nonhiring
IRS employees claim that a regulation titled "three considerations for appointment" is the reason for nonhiring--despite the regulation's providing no such reason. The claim is a diversion. It masks the immediate, unlawful dropping of applicant from the selection process, cheating him of lawful employment procedure.

The IRS's violation of law protected by a judge of the federal district court is an attack on public security from IRS violation of law. Public security from IRS violations requires public awareness of the violations abetted by a district court judge. Exposing their joint betrayal of public trust is a public service.

### Employment of an applicant with a former conviction
Certainly, the IRS is not required to employ an applicant with a former conviction. Nevertheless, no law, rule, or regulation bars such applicant from federal employment. Indeed, law provides for employment of such applicant based upon his suitability for the job he seeks. Therefore, law requires the IRS examine applicant suitability. If determined suitable, he is selected. If determined

unsuitable and not selected, law requires the IRS notify him of the nonselection and advise him of his right to respond, a right denied, violated, by the IRS's unlawful "failure to act." Law provides remedy for the "failure to act." Remedy is provided in federal district court, Judge McLaughlin's Court.

### Cover-up by the IRS's Directorate of Personnel Services

Employees of the Directorate of Personnel Services cover up their violations with misleading statements and outright lies. The entire Directorate, including Director, Richard J. Cronin, engages in unlawful nonhiring as standard practice. Unlawful employment practice portends unlawful practice in other IRS areas, e.g., corrupt tax treatment of the T.E.A. party, as will be shown.

### Omission of suitability negates right of MSPB appeal

The IRS unlawfully failed to determine suitability. Had determination been made, and had it been negative, the Merit Systems Protection Board (MSPB) has jurisdiction to review an appeal. Absent negative determination, the MSPB lacks jurisdiction, thus no right of MSPB appeal. The IRS's "failure to act" unlawfully removes applicant, omits suitability, and defrauds him of the right of MSPB appeal.

### "Failure to act" is pretext of a nonexistent application which conceals "conviction"

The Selecting Officer's "failure to act" is the pretext of a nonexistent application. In effect, it is the fraudulent concealment of the conviction stated in the application. Concealed conviction obscures the requirement for determining suitability. Had the Selecting Officer openly acknowledged "conviction," she could not have omitted the determination undetected. The "failure to act" is a legal wrong over which the Court, not the MSPB, has subject matter jurisdiction.

## Two IRS practices for rejecting applicant: lawful, and unlawful

IRS's two practices for rejecting an applicant are identified by nomenclature: (1) "nonselection," the lawful practice, and (2) "nonhiring, the unlawful practice. Nonselection requires determination of suitability. Nonhiring unlawfully omits suitability. The Selecting Officer, with her "failure to act," omits suitability, fails to notify applicant, and immediately drops applicant from the selection process, a silent, stealthy violation of lawful selection practice.

## Pro se plaintiff

Cheated of the determination--therefore defrauded of the right of MSPB appeal in the event of a negative determination--I, as pro se litigant, filed complaint in federal district court against the IRS's stealthy, unlawful nonhiring practice. The term "pro se" refers to an individual who represents himself in Court without aid of legal counsel.

## Conviction/Presidential pardon

In 1985, while employed at the Department of Defense, I pled guilty to mail fraud, resigned, and tried in court. Sentence was suspended on condition of probation, fines, restitution, and five weeks of community service. In December 2000, I was granted a full and unconditional Presidential pardon.

## Denying law, the IRS will argue in vain for MSPB jurisdiction

Law requires the Selecting Officer to initiate the process of determining suitability of the applicant for the job for which he applied. Failing to act on the application, the Selecting Officer failed to initiate the required determination, a violation of law. Only under a negative determination, does the MSPB have the jurisdiction to review a complaint against the nonhiring of an applicant who is not a federal employee. My complaint against the IRS's unlawful "failure to act" and omission of suitability is under the subject matter jurisdiction of the federal district court. The MSPB, lacking jurisdiction, has no part in this case.

### The IRS's false reason of "three considerations" for nonhiring
As a result of the Selecting Officer's "failure to act," applicant and application simply "vanish." Queried for the <u>reason</u> for nonhiring, IRS employees state that an applicant not selected after three considerations needn't be selected--a sham reason. An applicant not selected for the "reason" that he is not selected is circular reasoning, nonsense logic. Such reasoning obscures both the concealed "conviction" as reason, and the absence of suitability, an unabashed IRS fraud.

### Concealment: IRS lie of "three considerations" of applicant
The Selecting Officer, failing to acknowledge "conviction," intentionally conceals it. Concealed conviction and omission of suitability underlie the immediate, unlawful dropping of applicant from the selection process. Thus, the IRS fraudulently obstructs the applicant's right to compete for employment--a prohibited personnel practice. The IRS's claim that applicant needn't be selected after he was considered three times and not selected, is an IRS lie. It is a lie because the Selecting Officer processed <u>no</u> "considerations" as she well knows. "Three considerations" do not exist, as will be proved. Violating law for convenience and "efficiency," the IRS is an outlaw federal agency. Violating law, the IRS, in the person of the Selecting Officer, cheats applicant of the right to lawful employment procedure.

### The Office of Personnel Management (OPM) policy
The Office of Personnel Management (OPM) delegates authority to the IRS for selection of applicants. The IRS is thus a Delegated

Examining Unit (DEU) of the OPM. Law and OPM policy <u>require</u> suitability procedure applied to <u>all</u> applicants competing for employment, including those with a former conviction.

For convenience and "efficiency," employees of the IRS violate law and OPM policy. They omit suitability and immediately drop applicant from consideration, the IRS's unlawful method of non-hiring as standard practice.

### <u>A judge who evades her duty of review aids the IRS</u>

The history also includes the actions of Judge McLaughlin who evades her duty to review IRS unlawful personnel practice. She evades review by deception, by denying the subject matter jurisdiction assigned her Court by law. She will not be able to substantiate her denial. She can only weasel around it.

In support of her denial, she argues the IRS's deceptive, unlawful nonhiring practice is lawful. Thus, she argues on behalf of the IRS as "adjunct counsel for the defense," evincing an unethical, judicial bias in favor of the IRS. Despite her efforts, she cannot lawfully evade the subject matter jurisdiction assigned her Court by Constitution and statute. Evasion is fraud: she will dismiss on ground of issue preclusion--while deciding <u>no</u> issues of IRS violations to be precluded--a farce!

### <u>Judge McLaughlin attempts to establish MSPB jurisdiction</u>

Denying Court jurisdiction, Judge McLaughlin attempts to prove <u>administrative</u> (MSPB) jurisdiction. If she proves MSPB jurisdiction, she evades review. As proof, she cites three cases of MSPB jurisdiction as analogies to my case. The analogies are sheer fantasy, as will be shown.

She claims existence in my case of factual--albeit <u>invisible</u>--determination of suitability. Because invisible, it must be inferred to exist from an agency <u>action</u>. But the Selecting Officer's "failure to act" is a "nonaction." Suitability cannot be inferred from a nonaction. Nevertheless, on advice of the Able Assistant, Judge McLaughlin attempts to demonstrate its existence. The attempt fails as it must.

The procedure for determining suitability is absent in the three cases as it is in my case. The three cases, however, differ from my case in that they present <u>overt</u> agency action from which suitability <u>can</u> be inferred, therefore can be "constructed," therefore under MSPB jurisdiction. In my case, the Selecting Officer's "failure to act" absolutely eliminates overt agency action. Nothing subsequent the "failure to act," a silent fraud, provides overt agency action from which the determination of suitability can be inferred. Moreover, the Selecting Officer's "failure to act" itself provides a cause of action for <u>judicial</u>--not <u>administrative</u> (MSPB)--review. Pursuant to Constitution, statute, and precedent it is Judge McLaughlin's Court, not the MSPB, that has subject matter jurisdiction for review, as will be proved.

<u>Complaint not within the administrative (MSPB) appeals process</u>
The administrative (MSPB) appeals process applies primarily to the complaints of federal employees. It also applies to the complaints of applicants who are not federal employees but who are determined unsuitable. The MSPB has jurisdiction over their complaints which provides the right of MSPB appeal. I am not a federal employee, <u>not</u> determined unsuitable, therefore the MSPB has no jurisdiction over my complaint, meaning no right of MSPB appeal. Consequently, the MSPB is not the lawful venue for review of the IRS's unlawful omission of suitability. Venue is Judge McLaughlin's Court which has the subject matter jurisdiction for review assigned it by Constitution and statute.

<u>"Majesty of the law"</u>
By exposing the violations of the IRS, this writing exposes the machinations of Judge McLaughlin, a federal district court judge

who unlawfully evades review of a lawful "cause of action," protects the IRS in her self-interest, and, without scruple, brazenly denies the jurisdiction of her Court. She hides her machinations by designating the case "nonprecedential," does not publish it, instead buries it in the black hole of the Court's embarrassing cases.

Judges refer to their practice as the "majesty of the law." This writing will provide a look-see at the dark underbelly of that "majesty," as practiced by Judge McLaughlin.

# CHAPTER I

# EXPOSURE OF IRS DECEPTIVE, UNLAWFUL NONHIRING

### IRS violates employment suitability law

Omitting suitability in violation of law, IRS employees immediately drop, that is, remove from the employment process an applicant who states derogatory information (e.g., conviction) in his application. Violating the requirement for suitability and immediately removing applicant is time-saving, "efficient." "Efficiency" leads to "quality salary increase." Monetary reward for "efficiency" is sufficient motive for IRS employees to violate suitability law.

Exposure reveals the lies underlying the IRS's nonhiring practice. Lies include those of the Selecting Officer, Linda G. Sott who, under oath in her <u>Declaration</u> to the Court, claims lawful selection procedures are implemented, knowing they are not. False declaration under oath is perjury.

Exposure reveals the mendacity of IRS employees and Judge McLaughlin, who readily violate law in their self-interest. This writing alerts applicants and their attorneys to IRS violations of personnel law, and to the trickery of a district court judge who defends the IRS in order to dodge her lawful duty of review.

1

Violating law, IRS and Court betray public trust. They become the master while the taxpayer who pays their salaries becomes the servant, a topsy-turvy state of affairs, a threat to the individual's security from lawless government

## The IRS's administration of regulations

At title 5 of the Code of Federal regulations (5 C.F.R.) are stated the regulations that govern the recruitment of personnel. Employees of the IRS are charged with implementing the C.F.R. Instead, without scruple, in self-interest of convenience and "efficiency," they violate their charge and implement their deceptive, unlawful non-hiring practice.

## Unlawful nonhiring as standard practice

It is unthinkable that employees of the IRS violate the lawful procedures they publicly declare they implement. Unthinkable but true. Moreover, their violations are a firmly established practice at the Directorate of IRS Personnel Services defended, no less, by Director, Richard J. Cronin, as will be shown. The IRS unlawfully failed to determine suitability (5 C.F.R. 731.101).

Suitability is based upon investigation of the applicant's background to determine whether his employment will adversely affect "efficient service in the position applied for" (5 C.F.R. 731.202 (a) (1)). Despite the stated conviction, the IRS omitted the determination as to prevent appeal to the MSPB had the determination been "unsuitable" (5 C.F.R. 731.501(a)). Determination, however, may have been "suitable." Omitting determination, the IRS cheats applicant of the possibility of being determined suitable for the position for which he applied

## Examining suitability is not an extraordinary process

Examination of suitability is a routine, clerical procedure within the Selecting Officer's normal duties. The examination consists of verification of information provided by the applicant in response to a questionnaire issued by the OPM. Sott's immediate dropping of applicant from consideration unlawfully excludes the OPM from the selection process. She did so with her "failure to act," that is, her failure to take a personnel action, a silent scam, a violation under Title 5 of the United States Code (5 U.S.C.) at 5 U.S.C. 2302(b)(8)(A)(i).

### IRS employees profit from immediate, unlawful removal of applicant

The immediate, unlawful removal of applicant is in the self-interest of IRS employees because it is convenient, time-saving, therefore "efficient." Aside from mere convenience, "efficiency," albeit unlawful, rewards employees of the IRS's Directorate of Personnel Services with "quality salary increase." Reward for violation of law, the ideal, corrupt personnel practice by Directorate employees.

### Selecting Officer's "Failure to act"

Underlying Sott's deceptive practice is her "failure to act," i.e., pretense of a nonexistent application, in effect, her concealment of the stated conviction. Concealed conviction obscures the require ment for determining suitability (5 C.F.R. 731.202(b)(2)). Sott's "failure to act" is actually the immediate dropping of applicant from the selection process, a "legal wrong" for which the MSPB lacks jurisdiction for review--but for which statute provides judicial review (5 U.S.C. 702).

Concealment, a deceptive "nonaction," obstructs applicant's right to compete for employment, a prohibited personnel practice (5 U.S.C. 2302(b)(4)):

> Any employee who has authority to take, direct others to take, recommend, or approve any personnel action, shall not, with respect to such authority deceive or willfully obstruct any person with respect to such person's right to compete for employment.

3

## IRS employees above the law

Motivated by convenience, and "efficiency"--and "quality salary increase"--IRS employees, believing themselves above the law immune from penalty, violate law in their self-interest, standard practice at the Directorate of Personnel Services.

## Application for employment

In fall 1999, responding to an IRS want-ad, I applied for the seasonal, clerical position of Tax Examiner, grade GS-04. I met all requirements for the job, scoring 90.6 in the competitive exam, within the highest four percent of scores. I was not selected and not notified thereof. The failure to notify, a violation of 5 C.F.R. 731.402(a), is "without observance of procedure required by law" (5 U.S.C. 706(2)(D)).

## The IRS's "Employment Suitability Notice to Applicants"

The application for employment comprises some six pages of sample test questions and information regarding the competitive exam. The pages are white, printed in black ink. A single page is yellow, also printed in black ink. Attention is immediately drawn to the yellow page. It is titled "Employment Suitability Notice to Applicants" (ESNA). The ESNA emphasizes the requirement for determining the suitability of applicant for the job for which he applied (5 C.F.R. 731.202(a)(1)).

Under the heading "Suitability Review," the ESNA states, "[y]our application will be prescreened for suitability and referred to the Office of Personnel Management, Federal Investigation Processing Center [FIPC] for adjudication if there are material suitability issues indicated." The word "will" is directive. It is the IRS's positive declaration that the procedure of suitability will be implemented. The ESNA cites a list of suitability issues which includes convictions. Having stated "conviction" in the application, I expected the suitability procedure. After all a federal agency honors its word, or so I thought.

### The IRS reneges on its "word"

Despite "convictions" being a suitability issue stated in the ESNA, despite IRS statement that such issue <u>will</u> be referred to the OPM "for adjudication," nothing was referred, and nothing was adjudicated. Silence ensued, as though "conviction" did not exist. A "nonexistent" conviction is its concealment which cheats applicant of the right to the determination. Determination is indeed a <u>right</u> because it is required by law (5 C.F.R. 731. 101), a duty owed <u>every</u> applicant (56 A. 498, 500). The IRS boasts its integrity, yet reneges on its "word," violates law, and engages in a cover-up scheme of lies and deception. IRS integrity? Nonsense, rather IRS fraud.

Sott's concealment of the stated conviction is the ploy that "erases" the requirement for suitability. In lieu of pursuing suitability, Sott, with her "failure to act," implements the IRS's deceptive, unlawful nonhiring practice. Her readiness to violate lawful procedure shows no fear of penalty, which attests to the IRS's law-violating, nonhiring practice as normative.

Sott's "failure to act" is defined by statute as an "agency action" (5 U.S.C. 551(13)). As such, it is judicially reviewable: "person suffering legal wrong because of agency action . . . is entitled to judicial review thereof" (5 U.S.C. 702), original jurisdiction of the Court under 28 U.S.C. 1331.

### "Integrity" of the IRS and "three considerations"

It is inconceivable that the IRS, representing the integrity of the United States Government, permits its Selecting Officers to violate suitability law, unlawfully drop applicant from the selection process, and cover up their violations with the rehearsed lie of "three considerations." Sott's violations, defended by the Director of IRS Personnel Services, Richard J. Cronin, confirms unlawful nonhiring as standard practice, all the while IRS employees proclaim integrity. The ESNA, for all it's worth, may just as well be eliminated, sparing the taxpayer the cost of its printing.

## Lawful selection, unlawful nonhiring

Statute provides a single procedure for lawful selection of applicants. The procedure applies uniformly to all applicants whether or not they present derogatory information, e.g., "conviction." The procedure is stated at 5 U.S.C. 3318(a):

> The nominating or appointing authority shall select for appointment to each vacancy from the highest three eligibles [applicants] available for appointment on the certificate furnished under section 3317(a) of this title, unless objection to one or more of the individuals certified is made to, and sustained by, the Office of Personnel Management for proper and adequate reason under regulations prescribed by the Office.

IRS employees, sure of impunity, omit <u>objection</u>, <u>reason</u>, and OPM approval in violation of 3318(a). In order to disguise unlawful nonhiring as lawful, they refer to their unlawful nonhiring as "nonselection," the lawful procedure.

## I make no claim to being selected

Never in the litigation of this case did I claim I should have been selected. I claim the IRS's unlawful omission of suitability defrauded me of the <u>possibility</u> of being selected. Were I lawfully nonselected based on negative suitability with the right of MSPB appeal (5 C.F.R. 731.501(a)), I should have no complaint, no case.

## Errors in the litigation of the complaint

As a pro se litigant unfamiliar with legal process, I made errors in litigating my case, especially the failure to recognize the significance of the distinction between the Court's jurisdiction over the person and jurisdiction over the subject matter of the complaint. The errors, however, are not mine alone. Major error was committed by the Clerk of Court (Clerk), Eastern District of Pennsylvania.

For example, at one point, I was <u>required</u> to appeal a <u>lawful</u> MSPB dismissal to the United States Court of Appeals for the Federal Circuit (Fed. Cir.). Appealing a lawful dismissal is contradictory. Nevertheless, I appealed as required by way of the Clerk's Office, October 11, 2007 (2008-3059). The Clerk erroneously docketed the appeal at the Third Cir., thus delaying the process. Neither my nor the Clerk's error affect the validity of my complaint, a lawful "cause of action" (5 U.S.C. 702; 704).

### Judge McLaughlin's false claim of "issue preclusion"

Evading review, Judge McLaughlin resorts to deception: she dismisses the complaint, claiming "issue preclusion" as ground for dismissal, false claim. In fact, she dismissed on ground of lack of jurisdiction, therefore <u>not</u> settling the issue of IRS unlawful non-hiring practice. Issue preclusion applies to issues that are <u>settled</u> by a valid, final decision in a court of competent jurisdiction, and a party attempts to relitigate the issues under a later, different claim. Such attempt is not dismissed for lack of jurisdiction. Such attempt is barred--<u>precluded</u>--from relitigation. Failing to render a valid, final decision, she could not lawfully bar. Instead she dismissed for lack of jurisdiction, belying her claim of issue preclusion. Her Court has jurisdiction (28 U.S.C. 1331). She deceives. My claim remains undecided.

### Absent valid final decision, complaint not settled

Valid, final decision "settles the rights of parties with respect to the subject matter of the suit unless it is reversed or set aside" (291 N.W. 118, 121). Decision "ends the litigation on the merits and leaves nothing for the court to do but execute the judgment" (183 F. 2d 29, 31; 403 F. 2d 674, 678). This did not occur.

Judge McLaughlin, continually dismissing for lack of jurisdiction, made no final decision on the issues, e.g., IRS "failure to act" and omission of suitability. Issue preclusion does <u>not</u> apply to undecided issues. Therefore, she cannot lawfully claim issue preclusion.

7

Her claim is an attempt to deceive and she, dismissing for lack of jurisdiction rather than barring for issue preclusion, knows it.

Because the issues remain undecided, there is no second litigation. The initial litigation lawfully continues. Every claim by Judge McLaughlin to a final decision--while she dismisses for lack of jurisdiction--is false. Rather than admitting her Court's jurisdiction and settling the complaint, Judge McLaughlin denies Court jurisdiction, unethically argues on behalf of the IRS, and dismisses for lack of jurisdiction. Her claim of "issue preclusion" is a bald-faced lie, a brazen attempt to deceive. Her Court has jurisdiction under 28 U.S.C. 1331, as she very well knows. Her dismissal, an outright fraud, violates 28 U.S.C. 1331.

# CHAPTER 2

# SUITABILITY, SELECTION, JURISDICTION

### IRS violates suitability requirement

Every applicant competing for federal employment must be determined suitable for the job for which he applied (5 C.F.R. 731.202(a)(1)). Suitability issues include convictions. Moreover, suitability issues do <u>not</u> automatically require nonselection of applicant.

### Sott, the Selecting Officer, violates suitability process

Lawful nonselection requires the Selecting Officer to <u>object</u> to applicant for proper <u>reason</u> <u>sustained</u> by the OPM (5 U.S.C. 3318(a)). It is not Sott, the Selecting Officer, but the OPM that adjudicates suitability. Sott failed to act, i.e., failed to <u>object</u> for proper <u>reason</u> <u>sustained</u> by the OPM, thereby removing OPM from the process, a violation of 5 U.S.C. 3318(a). In order to evade review, Judge McLaughlin defends Sott's violations, arguing unethically on Sott's behalf.

## Suitability, required procedure for employment

If applicant is determined suitable he is selected. If determined unsuitable and not selected, he has the right of MSPB appeal (5 C.F.R. 731.103(g)). If he is not a federal employee, is not determined unsuitable, is not selected, he has no right of MSPB appeal (5 C.F.R. 731.501(a)). I am not a federal employee, not determined unsuitable, and not selected therefore no right of MSPB appeal (5 C.F.R. 1201.3(a)(7)). Sott's "failure to act" (5 U.S.C. 551(13)), which omits suitability--despite the stated conviction!--cheats applicant of that right. Sott's "failure to act," is a legal wrong, subject to judicial, not administrative (MSPB) review (5 U.S.C. 702)--cynically evaded by Judge McLaughlin.

## Arbitrary nonhiring

Lawful nonselection cannot result from Sott's "failure to act," i.e., failure to object for proper reason sustained by OPM (5 U.S.C. 3318(a)). Ignoring 5 U.S.C. 3318(a), Sott violates lawful selection procedure (5 U.S.C. 706(2)(A)).

## Sott's pretext of a nonexistent application conceals conviction

Sott's "failure to act" is the pretext of a nonexistent application, a deception. It is the fraudulent concealment of the critical fact stated in the application, i.e., "conviction." The "failure to act" underlies her fraudulent omission of suitability (5 C.F.R. 731.101) and immediate, unlawful dropping of applicant from the selection process (5 U.S.C. 2302 (b)(8))A)(i)). Concealment, as a personnel practice violates 18 U.S.C. 1001(c)(1)--defended by Judge McLaughlin.

## IRS defies lawful selection procedure

No law bars an applicant with a conviction from federal employment. Rather, law provides procedure for employment. Brazenly violating law, IRS employees, seeking "efficiency," immediately drop applicant and cover up his removal with lies, including Sott's perjury, as will be shown.

The IRS, violating 5 C.F.R. 731. 402(a), did not notify me of the nonhiring, Queried as to the reason for nonhiring, IRS employees claim the "rule of three" as reason, carefully omitting mention of "conviction." Mentioning "conviction" would reveal Sott's "failure to act" (5 U.S.C. 702), and failure to determine suitability, a violation of 5 C.F.R. 731.101.

### Failure to act, "rule of three," and reason for nonhiring

Sott, claiming the so-called "rule of three" (5 C.F.R. 332.405) as reason for "nonselection," covers up her "failure to act." The "rule" states that an applicant considered three times for selection and not selected, needn't be selected. Sott's "failure to act," however, means three considerations do not exist, her claim a lie. No lawful IRS action follows Sott's "failure to act." The lie of the "rule of three" as reason is standard practice at the IRS's Directorate of Personnel Services, as illustrated in the case of Lackhouse v. MSPB (Ch. 14, below). The judges in that case failed to examine the reason for Mr. Lackhouse's removal. Instead, they accepted the IRS's lie of "rule of three" as reason, resulting in the IRS's getting away with its unlawful removal of Mr. Lackhouse. In my case, Judge McLaughlin defends Sotts lie of the "rule of three" as reason for "nonselection" in order to evade her duty of review of a "lawful cause of action," namely, my complaint (5 U.S.C. 704).

### Director, IRS Personnel Services, defends unlawful omission of suitability

Richard J. Cronin, Director, IRS Personnel Services, defends Sott's unlawful failure to determine suitability. The omission of suitability, a violation, is standard practice when it benefits IRS employees. In his letter November 25, 2002 (Ch. 4, below), he repeats the standard lie of "three considerations" as reason for nonhiring. "Three considerations" do not exist as confirmed by my FOIA search (Ch. 5, below). The nonhiring, bypassing OPM, violates 5 U.S.C. 3318(a).

Cronin's defense of Sott confirms the unlawful omission of suitability and lie of "three considerations" as standard IRS practice. Sott's concealment of conviction and <u>failure</u> to refer the nonhiring to OPM are normative. Sott's violations provide a cause of action against the IRS that Cronin should defend in Court. Instead, Judge McLaughlin, in order to evade review, rescues him from defending the IRS by denying Court jurisdiction in violation of 28 U.S.C. 1331.

<u>A judge accepting lawless agency action is a danger to the public</u>
Unlawful nonhiring practiced by employees of IRS Directorate of Personnel Services is a lawful cause of action in federal district court (5 U.S.C. 702; 704). Evading review, Judge McLaughlin accepts their unlawful nonhiring. A judge entrusted to uphold law, who ignores law for convenience, opens the public to IRS and judicial wrongdoing. Betrayal of public trust is dangerous and troubling.

<u>Two established IRS employment processes, lawful</u>
<u>and unlawful</u>
Lawful nonselection is the IRS's <u>overt</u> process which requires <u>objection</u> to the applicant "for proper and adequate reason" <u>sustained</u> by the OPM (5 U.S.C. 3318(a)), notification to applicant of the action against him, and advising him of his right to respond (5 C.F.R. 731.402(a)). Unlawful nonhiring is the IRS's <u>covert</u> process, i.e., the "failure to act" on the application, a violation (5 U.S.C. 702).

In brief, Sott's "failure to act" comprises the immediate, unlawful dropping of applicant from consideration, the unlawful omission of suitability, and the omission of OPM from the employment process,

## Two judges and jurisdiction

The case was brought before two judges: first, Judge James T. Giles, then Judge Mary A. McLaughlin. Judge Giles did <u>not</u> dismiss for lack of jurisdiction. Rather, he applied the administrative doctrine of "exhaustion of administrative remedies" prior to judicial hearing. The Administrative Procedures Act (APA) however provides judicial, not administrative, review of wrongful agency action (5 U.S.C. 702). Thus, administrative remedies do not apply to my complaint. Nevertheless, I appealed to the administrative MSPB. Judge Giles will review my complaint after I "exhaust" nonexistent administrative remedies.

Subsequent their "exhaustion," I resumed the litigation at Court, Judge McLaughlin presiding. In sharp contrast to Judge Giles's acknowledgment of jurisdiction, Judge McLaughlin, from the outset, claimed lack of jurisdiction. Lack of jurisdiction is lack of power to decide the issues. If she "proves" lack of jurisdiction she evades review. She cannot so prove, and cannot lawfully evade.

Jurisdiction is assigned her Court by U. S. Constitution, statute (28 U.S.C. 1331), and U.S. Supreme Court precedent (<u>Califano v. Sanders</u>, 430 U.S. 99, 105 (1977), hereinafter <u>Califano v. Sanders</u>.) Therefore, she cannot "prove" lack of jurisdiction. She can only resort to deception to deny it, and dismissal by fiat to evade it. She cannot credibly deny her Court's original jurisdiction.

Evading review, Judge McLaughlin argues as "adjunct counsel for the defense" on behalf of the IRS. She defends Sott's unlawful "failure to act" (5 U.S.C. 702) and concealment of "conviction. Sott's personnel practice of concealment is a violation (18 U.S.C. 1001(c)(1)). She defends the IRS's unlawful omission of <u>objection</u> for proper <u>reason</u> <u>sustained</u> by the OPM (5 U.S.C. 3318(a)). She defends Sott's failure to pursue suitability (5 C.F.R. 731.101) and immediate, unlawful dropping applicant from employment process. Evading Court jurisdiction, she argues for nonexistent MSPB jurisdiction. Her drive to evade review of a lawful cause of action that she cannot lawfully evade is obsessive, not rational.

## Evasion of review: shared goal of the IRS and Judge McLaughlin

Evasion of review well serves IRS employees and Judge McLaughlin. IRS employees seek to avoid review because they cannot validly defend their unlawful nonhiring practice in Court. Judge McLaughlin's motive is unknown. Perhaps she has an aversion to pro se litigants. Perhaps she believes IRS violations trivial, with review cutting into her time on the golf course. What is known, because it is obvious, is her trickery to disprove the jurisdiction assigned her Court by law.

## U.S. Supreme Court and Third Cir. affirm Court jurisdiction

The United States Supreme Court, under Pub. Law 94-574, 90 Stat. 2721, enacted by Congress October 21, 1976, held that 28 U.S.C. 1331 confers "jurisdiction on federal courts to review agency action." It stated, "it is common ground that, if review is proper under the APA, the District Court had jurisdiction under 28 U.S.C. § 1331." Bowen v. Massachusetts, 487 U.S. 879, 891 n 16 (1988). (Hereinafter Bowen v. Massachusetts.)

## Third Circuit affirms Court jurisdiction

The United States Court of Appeals for the Third Cir. held, "under the APA (5 U.S.C. 701-706), federal courts have jurisdiction to review . . . under 28 U.S.C. 1331 . . ." actions arising "under the APA." (See Yeboah v. Department of Justice Immigration and Naturalization Service, 345 F. 3d 216, Third Cir. 2003, hereinafter Yeboah v. DOJ). The Third Cir. is the court Judge McLaughlin first claims lacks jurisdiction, then later claims has jurisdiction.

The APA provides, "[a] person suffering legal wrong because of agency action" or failure to take action "is entitled . . . to judicial review" (5 U.S.C. 702). There is no doubt that Judge McLaughlin's

Court has subject matter jurisdiction for review of a lawful "cause of action" (5 U.S.C. 704), namely, my complaint.

## Judge McLaughlin's false ground of "issue preclusion" for dismissal

Judge McLaughlin eventually dismissed the complaint claiming ground of issue preclusion--but in fact dismissed on "ground" of lack of jurisdiction, a change of ground, a brazen attempt to deceive. The two grounds do not lawfully coexist. Dismissing for lack of jurisdiction while her Court holds original jurisdiction is dismissal by fiat, outright fraud by a district court judge.

## IRS's defense counsel, the Department of Justice (DOJ), obfuscates

Attorneys of the Department of Justice (DOJ) are the IRS's defense counsel. They defend the Selecting Officer's "failure to act" (5 U.S.C. 551(13)), i.e., the failure to take a personnel action, a violation of 5 U.S.C. 2302(b)(8)(A)(i). The "failure to act" is, in fact, the omission of suitability, a violation of 5 C.F.R. 731.101. The omission, Sott's fraud, obstructs the right to compete for employment, a prohibited personnel practice, a violation of 5 U.S.C. 2302(b)(4).

Sott's "failure to act," and omission of suitability are violations of law that go directly to the merits of my complaint. The DOJ defends the violations by obscuring them. DOJ attorneys create incongruous concepts such as "merits of suitability," a meaningless term intended to obscure the issues. The term "merits" applied to suitability is an oxymoron. "Merits" applies solely to the issues of IRS violations. DOJ's "merits of suitability" is double-talk fakery, to confuse.

## DOJ attorneys defend Sott's "failure to act"

Defending Sott's "failure to act," the DOJ defends Sott's concealment of the critical fact stated in the application, namely, "conviction." The concealment, a fraud, alters the critical content of the application and underlies Sott's unlawful omission of suitability. Sott's practice of concealment, a violation (18 U.S.C. 1001(c)(1), defended by the DOJ. The DOJ ("J" for justice) defends a crooked IRS. Justice? DOJ attorneys are laughing themselves silly.

# CHAPTER 3

# IRS UNLAWFULLY "ERASES" SUITABILITY

### Sott's failure to act "erases" suitability

In response to the application, Sott, the Selecting Officer, unlawfully failed to act (5 U.S.C. 551(13)), the pretext of a nonexistent application subject to judicial review (5 U.S.C. 702). Failing to act, she concealed the stated conviction. "Conviction" is a criterion for determining suitability (5 C.F.R. 731.202(b)(2)). Concealing conviction, she "erases" both criterion and suitability, a convenient, time-saving ploy, resulting in the "efficiency" which leads to IRS quality salary increase. "Erasing" the requirement for suitability violates 5 C.F.R. 731.101.

### Absent unsuitability means absent right of MSPB appeal

The "individual who has been found unsuitable may appeal the finding to the Merit Systems Protection Board (the Board)" (5 C.F.R. 731.501(a)). Because Sott failed to act, I was not "found unsuitable," thus no right of MSPB appeal. Moreover, Sott's unlawful "failure to act" is not within the MSPB's administrative process. It is within the judicial process, to be reviewed by Judge McLaughlin (5 U.S.C. 702).

## FOIA search for reason for nonhiring (Bossert, Cronin, Behm)

Suitability procedure provides the possibility of employment. Consequently, I sought to ascertain the reason for its absence and for the nonhiring. I was certain the reason was "conviction" stated in the application. If a different reason, the IRS did not state it. Nonhiring absent a substantive reason fails the smell test.

Pursuant to the Freedom of Information Act (FOIA), I embarked upon a two-year attempt to uncover the reason for the nonhiring. I corresponded with a number of individuals involved in IRS personnel practice. Three of the individuals directly relate to the reason for nonhiring: Barbara A. Bossert, Acting Chief, Recruitment Section, Philadelphia, PA (January 9, 2001); Richard J. Cronin, Director, IRS Personnel Services, Washington, D.C, (November 25, 2002); Richard L. Behm, IRS Riverside Appeals Office, Riverside, CA, (December 16, 2003).

## Ms. Bossert's response

By letter dated 9 January 2001, I requested Ms. Bossert provide the specific, substantive reason for my rejection, and the percentage or number of selectees who scored lower than I on the competitive examination. Her response (letter dated 5 February 2001) was evasive. She provided neither the specific, substantive reason for nonhiring, nor the percentage or number of selectees with scores lower than mine. I later learned approximately ninety-six percent of selectees scored lower than my score of 90.6. Not one word in her letter referred to "conviction" as reason.

## Bossert "indicates" the regulation "rule of three" as reason for nonhiring

Bossert stated, "5 CFR 332.405 indicates that an agency will select in accordance with the Rule of Three." This is not a specific, substantive reason, only a vague "indicates." Vague response is hiding something, possibly "conviction" as reason? The term "indicates" is an obfuscation, an attempt to deceive.

The "rule of three" ("rule") adopted in 1871 requires selection of the highest scoring applicant from each group of three highest scoring applicants listed sequentially highest to lowest score. Bossert believes the "rule of three" to be regulation 5 C.F.R. 332.405. It reads as follows:

> An appointing officer [Selecting Officer] is not required to consider an eligible who has been considered by him for three separate appointments from the same or different certificates for the same position.

The title of the regulation is, however, not "rule of three." The title is "Three considerations for appointment." Also, the regulation does not define the term "consideration." Thus, "consideration" may be Sott contemplating her navel, deciding whom to select. "Consideration" is, in fact, the process of suitability. It comprises objection to applicant for reason sustained by the OPM. Bossert fails to state "three considerations" were actually implemented. In fact, they were not, which will be proved. Bossert is aware of the absence of "three considerations" and brazenly lies. Lying is necessary for defending the IRS's deceptive, unlawful nonhiring practice. Unlawful personnel practice cannot be truthfully defended.

The essence of 5 C.F.R. 332.405 is, an applicant who is not selected after three considerations, needn't be selected--nonsense logic, cause and effect being the same. That is, an applicant thrice not hired (cause) needn't be hired (result). Bossert conceals the objective reason of "conviction" as cause. Stating a "rule" that "indicates" nonhiring, she deceives. Bossert, omitting conviction as reason, obscures Sott's "failure to act," the unlawful dropping of applicant from the selection process.

<u>The "rule of three," 5 C.F.R. 332.405, and 5 U.S.C. 3318(a)</u>
Regulation 5 C.F.R. 332.405, <u>indicated</u> by Bossert as reason for nonhiring, is falsely referred to as the "rule of three" because it omits the substance of the actual "rule of three" stated at 5 U.S.C. 3318(a). Substance is the act of objecting to applicant for "adequate and proper reason" sustained by the OPM. Absent the substance, Sott's nonhiring is "arbitrary, capricious, an abuse of discretion, or otherwise not in accordance with law" (5 U.S.C. 706(2)(A)). Bossert's term "indicates," is a weasel-word deception, the IRS's corrupt stock-in-trade.

While Bossert and Sott refer to 5 C.F.R. 332.405 as the "rule of three," the OPM refers to 5 U.S.C. 3318(a) as the lawful <u>implementation</u> of the "rule of three": "[t]raditionally, applicants for Federal jobs are assigned numerical scores including veterans' preference points, if appropriate, and are considered for selection based on the 'rule of three' (5 U.S.C. 3318(a))." (See http:/www. opm.gov/ fedregis/2004/6906154-33272-a.htm.)

How is it that the OPM cites 5 U.S.C. 3318(a), which requires <u>objection</u> for <u>reason</u> <u>sustained</u> by the OPM as being <u>based</u> on the "rule of three," while Bossert and Sott cite 5 C.F.R. 332.405--which omits 3318(a)--<u>is</u> the "rule of three"? Answer: the OPM, with nothing to hide, states the substance of the "rule of three," while Bossert and Sott, with everything to hide, cite 5 C.F.R. 332.405 to obscure the substance of the "rule of three," i.e., <u>objection</u> for <u>reason</u> <u>sustained</u> by OPM.

Moreover, the wording at 5 C.F.R. 332.405, which lacks the substance of 5 U.S.C. 3318(a), provides no evidence of three considerations as having been implemented. In addition, 5 C.F.R. 332.405 is silent regarding the elements of a lawful consideration. It provides no rationale for the necessity of three considerations. It merely refers to three considerations.

Sott conceals "conviction," omits suitability, immediately drops applicant from consideration violating 5 U.S.C. 3318(a). Had she mentioned "conviction," she would have had to pursue the suitability determination she unlawfully omitted.

### Deception of "three considerations"

Bossert deceives with her "indication" that the Selecting Officer actually processed "three considerations." Pursuant to FOIA, information provided by the IRS's Riverside Appeals Office, Riverside, CA, confirms the <u>absence</u> of "three considerations," as will be shown. No "considerations" were processed. Bossert's allusion to "three considerations" is the standard, reflex lie constantly repeated at the IRS's Directorate of Personnel Services. Sott's response is typical of the misleading statements made by employees of the Directorate. They are unable to function without deceiving. There, the rot of deception is bone deep.

### 5 C.F.R. 332.405 lacks the substance of 5 C.F.R. 332.406(a)

The substance lacking in 5 C.F.R. 332.405 is provided under 5 C.F.R. 332.406(a), titled "Objections to eligible," which states, in part, the following:

> An appointing officer is not required to consider an eligible to whose certification for the particular position he makes an objection that is sustained by OPM for any of the reasons stated in . . . [5 C.F.R.] 731.201.

Instead of <u>objection</u> <u>sustained</u> by the OPM, there is Sott's "failure to act," meaning no <u>objection</u>, no <u>reason</u>, and nothing <u>sustained</u> by the OPM, therefore no "three considerations." Sott, echoed by Bossert, both claiming "three considerations," reveals them as brazen liars, a quality in ample supply at the Directorate of Personnel Services. Sott processed not one, let alone "three considerations," and Bossert, as Acting Chief, Recruitment Section, knows it.

Regulation 5 C.F.R. 332.406(a), ignored by Sott, makes it perfectly clear that the so-called "rule" 5 C.F.R. 332.405 is empty of substance, yet Sott claims it as authority for lawful "nonselection," attempting to deceive. The so-called "rule" is, in effect, a half-regulation, the other half being 5 C.F.R. 332.406(a). Were the two regulations combined, Sott could not have avoided suitability. Two regulations that should be one, an IRS ploy as cover for the unlawful omission of suitability.

## Competitive selection procedure

Employment in the competitive service requires applicants be ranked sequentially, highest to lowest score. Offer of employment is made to the applicant with the highest score at each succeeding selection from the three highest scoring applicants. In the event the highest scoring applicant is not selected, the Selecting Officer is required to <u>object</u> to his employment for proper <u>reason</u> <u>sustained</u> by the OPM (5 U.S.C. 3318(a)).

Sott, violating 3318(a), selected applicants with scores lower than mine while failing to provide a reason for so doing <u>sustained</u> by OPM. Sott, giving "any preference or advantage not authorized by law, rule, or regulation to any . . . applicant for employment . . . for the purpose of . . . injuring the prospects of any particular person for employment" is a prohibited personnel practice (5 U.S.C. 2302(b)(6)). Selecting applicants who scored lower than I, absent <u>objection</u> and <u>reason,</u> <u>sustained</u> by OPM injured--deleted--my prospects for employment. This prohibited personnel practice is defended by Richard J. Cronin, Director, IRS Personnel Services.

## Deceptive, unlawful nonhiring v. lawful nonselection

Defending her deceptive nonhiring, Sott lies, even to the extent of making misleading <u>declarations</u> to the Court under oath--perjury--ignored by Judge McLaughlin. She frames her lies in the terminology of law. Applying the term "nonselection," i.e., the lawful procedure of 5 U.S.C. 3318(a), to the IRS's unlawful nonhiring practice, Sott disguises deceptive nonhiring as lawful.

An applicant subjected to the IRS's "failure to act," is not lawfully "nonselected." He is immediately, unlawfully dropped from the selection process in violation of 5 C.F.R. 731.101. Labeling his unlawful removal a nonselection, IRS employees deceive. They cannot defend their violations without deceiving.

### Cover-up of three nonexistent considerations

Sott <u>failed to act</u>, i.e., failed to <u>object</u>, failed to state a <u>reason</u> <u>sustained</u> by the OPM in violation of 5 C.F.R. 332.406(a). She failed to notify applicant of the nonhiring and his right to respond, a violation of 5 C.F.R. 731.402. Sott's failures puts the lie to her claim of existent "three considerations," and to every IRS claim of lawful selection procedure. Her claim of implementing "three considerations" is a bald-faced lie. Invoking the so-called "rule of three" as reason for nonhiring, Sott augments her concealment of the conviction I stated in my application. Bossert, referring to the so-called "rule of three" joins with Sott's lie.

With her "failure to act," Sott was the first to conceal the stated conviction. Bossert's claim of "three considerations" while omitting reference to "conviction" is the second concealment. IRS employees, acting in self-interest, able to violate law with impunity, are a threat to public safety from lawless government. Their trashing the law without fear of penalty is a perfect abuse of power--and an outrage. They must be exposed and penalized.

Bossert is aware that selection of a lower-scoring in place of a higher scoring applicant must comply with 5 U.S.C. 3318(a). Yet she joins with Sott's claim of "rule of three" (5 C.F.R. 332.405) as <u>reason</u> for nonhiring--while knowing Sott concealed "conviction" as reason in violation of 3318(a). IRS employees violate lawful procedure and lie as though they have the right to do so. Their lies defended by Director of Personnel Services, Richard J. Cronin, it seems they have that "right."

### "Failure to act" delegitimizes every subsequent IRS claim to lawful procedure

It is indisputable that Sott failed to act on the application, thereby unlawfully omitting objection, reason, three considerations, and suitability in violation of 5 U.S.C. 3318(a). Consequently, no personnel procedure subsequent her "failure to act" complies with the requirements of lawful nonselection. Every claim she makes to lawful employment procedure subsequent her "failure to act" is false.

# CHAPTER 4

# DIRECTOR, PERSONNEL SERVICES DEFENDS LACK OF SUITABILITY

### Director Cronin's response: suitability irrelevant?

In response to my query of "conviction" as reason for nonhiring, Richard J. Cronin, Director, IRS Personnel Services, in his letter dated November 25, 2002, stated, "[t]here was never an attempt to object, or remove you . . . based on suitability for employment." True, and an admission of wrongful agency action--in face of "conviction" which <u>requires</u> determination of suitability, unlawfully omitted! Not "conviction" but the standard lie of "rule of three" as reason? The brazen gall of it. Cronin actually defends the unlawful omission of suitability.

He claims that I was "considered three times, but not selected from this certificate and then removed from further consideration." He repeats Sott's and Bossert's lie of the "rule of three" as <u>reason</u> for my removal--knowing three considerations do not exist! Defending the lie of "three considerations," Director Cronin facilitates the IRS's deceptive, unlawful nonhiring practice.

In face of the stated conviction, does he truly believe suitability is irrelevant? This cannot be, which is why he alludes to it. Of course it is relevant--critical to selection. If, however, he indeed believes suitability irrelevant, he must believe its omission is lawful. If so, he should be relieved of his position for incompetence.

### Unlawful omission of suitability, a necessary fraud

Omission of suitability is necessary for fraudulent nonhiring. Therefore Cronin defends Sott's failure to pursue suitability which the IRS stated in its ESNA would be pursued. Instead, implementing the IRS's fraudulent nonhiring practice, he repeats the standard lie of "three considerations" as reason for nonhiring. He promotes and participates fully in IRS fraudulent nonhiring, standard practice at the Directorate of Personnel Services. The Directorate, corrupt from top to bottom.

### FOIA confirms absence of "three considerations"

Pursuant to my FOIA request, the IRS confirmed it has no record-- no evidence--of three considerations. Absence of three considerations belies Sott's and Cronin's brazen claim of the so-called "rule of three" (5 C.F.R 332.405) as reason for nonhiring. Their concealment of the stated conviction is outright fraud. Believing themselves above the law, IRS employees without hesitation violate law if perceived in their self-interest. Lying, arrogance, and contempt for law their standard, all the while proclaiming IRS "integrity."

### Director's "authority" for deceptive, unlawful nonhiring

As Director of IRS Personnel Services, Cronin is aware of the requirement for suitability (5 C.F.R. Part 731). He is aware that omission of suitability is necessary for unlawful nonhiring. This raises the question of his "authority" for nonhiring, absent the determination of applicant's suitability.

"Authority" does not stem from law but from the IRS's manual of practice, the Internal Revenue Manual (IRM), Part 6, which is not law. The relevant practice is stated at IRM 6.331.1.20, duplicitously worded, self-contradictory, and unlawful.

IRM 6.331.1.20 states," in part, as follows:

> IRS offices should pursue a suitability determination if the applicant's circumstances meet the established criteria [e.g., conviction] for referral, rather than simply 'non selecting' and working within the 'rule of three' for consideration (see 6.331.1.21 below). Please refer to 5 CFR 731 and IRM 6.731 for further guidance.

### IRM 6.331.1.20, a duplicitous nonhiring practice

On one hand, the word "should" <u>directs</u> pursuit of the determination (5 C.F.R. 731.101). On the other hand, the word "rather" actually provides the <u>choice</u> of "simply 'non selecting' and working within the 'rule of three' for consideration," a violation of 5 U.S.C. 3318(a). The unlawful practice of "simply non selecting," which omits <u>objection</u> and <u>reason</u> <u>sustained</u> by the OPM, has been implemented in previous, deceptive IRS nonhirings, as illustrated in the <u>Lackhouse</u> cases (Ch. 14, below).

IRM 6.331.1.20 is self-contradictory in that it provides the Selecting Officer with the choice of pursuing either lawful suitability (5 C.F.R. 731.101), or unlawful "simply non selecting" which is, in fact, "failure to act" (5 U.S.C. 702). Because IRM 6.331.1.20 does not prohibit the deceptive practice of "simply non selecting," the Selecting Officer's choosing it is rational--but unlawful. Sott, the Selecting Officer, chose "simply non selecting," i.e., "failure to act," in effect, the immediate, unlawful dropping of applicant from the selection process.

The phrase "working within the 'rule-of-three' for consideration" underlies Sott's use of 5 C.F.R. 332.405 as the fraudulent <u>reason</u> for nonhiring, That is, conceal conviction, fail to act, and claim 5 C.F.R. 332.405 as <u>reason</u>. "Working within the 'rule-of-three' for consideration" is deception, the attempt to present unlawful non-hiring as lawful. "Working within" means "scheming to nonhire."

Duplicitous wording of IRM 6.331.1.20 exemplifies IRS corrupt practice. Seeking efficiency and salary increase, IRS employees resort to time-saving, i.e., "efficient"--but unlawful--omission of suitability. Thus, they defraud applicant of the right to the determination of suitability. Able to violate law with impunity they make the IRS an outlaw federal agency, a threat to public well-being. Public security requires exposure of corrupt IRS practices.

### Selecting Officer disregards IRM 6.331.1.21

While IRM 6.331.1.20 provides rationale for "simply non selecting"--i.e., the immediate, unlawful removal of applicant--it also directs attention to IRM 6.331.1.21. IRM 6.331.1.21 refers to 5 U.S.C. 3318, which requires objection to applicant, for reason sustained by the OPM (5 U.S.C. 3318(a)).

Had Sott, the Selecting Officer complied with IRM 6.331.1.21, she would have had to comply with 5 U.S.C. 3318(a) by pursuing suitability and proceeding with lawful nonselection. Instead, she ignores 6.331.1.21 and engages in "simply 'non selecting' and working within the 'rule of three' for consideration," the IRS's deceptive, unlawful nonhiring practice.

Sott, failing to comply with IRM 6.331.1.21, omits objection and reason for nonhiring, a violation of 5 U.S.C. 3318(a). "Simply non selecting" unlawfully "erases" the requirement for the determination of suitability (5 C.F.R. 731.101). While fully aware of "conviction" stated in the application, Sott fails to act, a brazen violation of 5 U.S.C. 2302(b)(8)(A)(i).

### Selecting Officer's "failure to act" underlies lawless procedure

Because the "failure to act," i.e., "simply non select," is Sott's first unlawful "agency action," no subsequent, lawful selection procedure is possible. Defense of IRS deceptive, unlawful nonhiring is only by deception. Every IRS argument in defense of its nonhiring practice is fraudulent. The IRS, a massive agency bloated with 90,000 employees, that violates law with impunity, is an outlaw agency that trashes citizens' rights. Exposing IRS corruption is protective of citizens' rights.

### "Nonexistent conviction" and deceptive nonhiring practice

Sott's pretense of a nonexistent conviction for evading suitability begins with her "failure to act." Ignoring the stated conviction, she failed to <u>object</u>, <u>failed</u> to provide proper <u>reason</u> <u>sustained</u> by the OPM, <u>failed</u> to pursue suitability, and <u>failed</u> to select the highest score from the three highest scoring eligibles, a violation of 5 U.S.C. 3318(a)). Sott's pretense is defended by Director, Richard J. Cronin who runs a law-violating Directorate in which deception is standard practice.

### "Bait and switch" swindle

The IRS's nonhiring practice is a scam. It even has the earmarks of a bait and switch swindle. The bait is the IRS's "word" of pursuing suitability stated in its ESNA. The switch is the IRS's unscrupulous reneging on its word, unlawfully <u>omitting</u> suitability, business as usual at the Directorate of Personnel Services.

### IRM 10.23.3.1, the "corrective" to the duplicity of 6.331.1.20

Possibly a result of my complaint of IRS unlawful omission of suitability, a "corrective" to the duplicitous 6.331.1.20 is the recently created IRS directive, IRM 10.23.3.1 (04-17-2008, paragraph 3), which states the following:

> Suitability determinations <u>must</u> [emphasis added] be made when derogatory information [conviction] about an applicant or employee surfaces in the course of preemployment or background investigations.

The directive reveals IRS sensitivity to my complaint of IRS nullification of suitability procedure and deceptive nonhiring covered up with the ruse of "simply 'non selecting' and working within the 'rule-of-three' for consideration" (IRM 6.331.1.20). Based on IRS genius for deception, nothing guarantees IRS implementation of 10.23.3.1. Exposure may help constrain IRS corruption.

IRM 10.23.3.1 also states, "[b]ackground investigations . . . constitute the first step in the process of ensuring the highest standards of honesty, integrity, and security among (IRS) employees." IRS employees and integrity? They violate law and lie while they proclaim it. Absent exposure and punishment, IRS employees will continue with their corrupt personnel practice when perceived in their self-interest.

In addition to violating personnel law for convenience and "efficiency," IRS employees violate tax law for political self-purpose. Thus, they harass and subject to prejudicial tax treatment the T.E.A. Party, a grass-roots group dedicated to uphold the U. S. Constitution. The Director of IRS Exempt Organizations Division who doesn't care a fig for the Constitution is the harasser. Accused of unlawful practice, she pled the Fifth Amendment before Congress May 10, 2013, and resigned--with full pension!--a rip-off of the taxpayer, with contempt for the taxpayer.

# CHAPTER 5

# FOIA SEARCH: ABSENCE OF "THREE CONSIDERATIONS"

### FOIA search ended, Mr. Behm's response

The search for the reason for my nonhiring ended December 16, 2003 with the written response of Mr. Richard L. Behm, IRS Riverside Appeals Office, Riverside, CA, 92506. He advised that the IRS Disclosure Office stated, "no additional records which are responsive to your request" [the reason for nonnhiring], i.e., no record of "three considerations." Had there been a lawful non-selection, record of "considerations," namely, <u>objection</u> for <u>reason sustained</u> by the OPM would exist. Absence of record reveals the claim by IRS, DOJ, and Judge McLaughlin of "three considerations" underlying the nonhiring as the lie that it is.

Every response by IRS employees to the many requests for the reason for nonhiring is the so-called "rule of three"--while they know "three considerations" do not exist. Absence of "three considerations" confirms fraudulent nonhiring as standard IRS practice, a violation of 5 U.S.C. 3318(a)).

The Selecting Officer's "failure to act," her concealment of "conviction," her lie of the so-called "rule of three" as <u>reason</u> for nonhiring, her omission of "suitability," and her immediate dropping of applicant from the selection process are deceptive "agency actions" that obstruct the applicant's right to compete for employment. Obstruction by deception of the right to compete is a "prohibited personnel practice" (5 U.S.C. 2302(b)(4))--defended by Judge McLaughlin!

### MSPB lacks jurisdiction to review a nonadministrative appeal

The 1978 Civil Service Reform Act (CSRA) assigned the task of review of administrative appeals to the MSPB (5 C.F.R. 1201.3).

The MSPB has jurisdiction over complaints of individuals who are in the administrative appeals process, namely, federal employees. I am not a federal employee, therefore no MSPB jurisdiction. In my case, MSPB jurisdiction and right of appeal exist solely in the event of a negative determination of suitability (5 C.F.R. 1201. 3(a)(7)). Sott, unlawfully omitting suitability, nullified right of MSPB appeal, shielding the IRS from appeal had I been determined unsuitable.

### Prewitt v. MSPB, "failure to act"

Furthermore, Sott's unlawful "failure to act" itself negates the right of MSPB appeal: "failure to select an applicant for the vacant position is generally not appealable to the Board" (Prewitt v. Merit Systems Protection Board, 133 F.3d 885, 886 (Fed. Cir. 1988)) (hereinafter Prewitt v. MSPB). Consequently, appeal to the MSPB is pointless, to be dismissed for lack of jurisdiction.

The lawful venue for review of Sott's "failure to act" (5 U.S.C. 551(13)) is the judiciary, namely, federal district court. Pursuant to the APA, "[a] person suffering legal wrong because of agency action . . . is entitled to judicial review thereof" (5 U.S.C. 702), Court jurisdiction under 28 U.S.C. 1331.

# CHAPTER 6

# FILING THE COMPLAINT (04-4876)

"Failure to act" negates MSPB jurisdiction

"Three considerations" do not exist. IRS employees' claim of the so-called "rule of three" as reason for nonhiring, is a brazen, cynical lie. Their claim reveals an agency where lying is normative, part of the job. Because the MSPB lacks jurisdiction, and my complaint being a lawful "cause of action" (5 U.S.C. 704), on date October 24, 2004, I filed my complaint of IRS deceptive, unlawful nonhiring practice at federal district court (Civil Action 04-4876, hereinafter 04-4876), Judge James T. Giles presiding. The complaint comprises the IRS's unlawful nonhiring practice:

1. "Failure to act" (5 U.S.C. 551(13)), to be reviewed by the Court (5 U.S.C. 702)
2. "Failure to take a personnel action regarding "conviction," a violation of (5 U.S.C. 2302(b)(8)(A)(i)
3. Failure of the Selecting Officer to <u>object</u> to applicant for proper <u>reason</u> <u>sustained</u> by the OPM, a violation of 5 U.S.C. 3318(a)
4. Failure of the IRS to determine suitability, a violation of 5 C.F.R. 731.101

5. Negation of the MSPB's jurisdiction for review due to the Selecting Officer's failure to determine unsuitability (5 C.F.R. 731.501(a))
6. The deceptive practice at IRM 6.331.1.20 of "simply non selecting" omitting suitability, is "without observance of procedure required by law" (5 U.S.C. 706(2)(D))
7. The Selecting Officer's claim of the "rule of three" (5 C.F.R. 332.405) as <u>reason</u> for the nonhiring--despite the fact it provides no such reason is therefore a lie
8. Sott's lie, under oath, of "three considerations" knowing she did not process them, perjury, a felony (18 U.S.C. 1621)
9. The IRS's overall violation of due process

## IRS Motion to dismiss

Responding to the complaint, IRS counsel for the defense, namely, attorneys of the DOJ, on date April 8, 2005, filed a <u>Motion to Dismiss</u> (hereinafter <u>Motion 04-4876</u>), based on the following arguments:

1a. The complaint must be dismissed as the IRS use of the rule of three is not abuse of discretion
2a. Plaintiff fails to state a claim against defendant under "rule of three" due to his failure to appeal to MSPB
3a. Plaintiff complaint must be dismissed for failure to exhaust his administrative remedies

## DOJ's so-called "abuse of discretion"

The "abuse of discretion" standard, as it applies to an administrative agency, concerns the agency's lawful discretion to perform a prescribed action. For example, an agency that holds <u>discretionary</u> authority to issue a license, but refuses to do so, may be abusing its discretion, thus subject to Court review.

First, the DOJ misleads by linking "use of the rule of three" with abuse of discretion. Three considerations do not exist as confirmed by the FOIA search. Implying their "use," the DOJ deceives. Moreover, the IRS has <u>no</u> discretion to omit three considerations. Their omission violates 5 U.S.C. 3318(a).

"Abuse of discretion" argument is intended to obfuscate. "Discretion" has no connection with the "rule of three." Conflating "rule of three" with "discretion" diverts attention from Sott's concealed "conviction" and obscures IRS unlawful omission of suitability. DOJ argument is a deceptive defense of IRS violation of suitability law. Defending the lie of three considerations, DOJ attorneys obfuscate because they cannot validly defend IRS violation of 5 U.S.C. 3318(a).

### Failure to state a claim under "rule of three," a DOJ obfuscation

Second, Sott failed to act, a violation. "Three considerations" and MSPB jurisdiction do not exist, reference to them a DOJ obfuscation. Determination of suitability is required (5 C.F.R. 731.101). Therefore I have a right to it, and have so claimed. DOJ arguing, "[p]laintiff fails to state a claim . . ." is obfuscation.

### DOJ states "exhaust administrative remedies"

Third, absent determination of <u>unsuitability</u>, administrative remedies do not exist (5 C.F.R. 731.501(a)). Venue for complaint of IRS "failure to act" is the Court, for which the APA provides <u>judicial</u> not administrative (MSPB) review (5 U.S.C. 702). Court jurisdiction under 28 U.S.C. 1331. MSPB has no role here.

### Nonprocedure, suitability, arbitrary nonhiring

Regarding "discretion" and the requirement for suitability, DOJ, at page 9 of <u>Motion 04-4876</u>, fabricates a false procedure--actually, a "nonprocedure." That is, "[Selecting Officer] was not required to prepare a written determination or provide any type of record of explanation as to why one candidate was selected over another." The argument is bizarre, utterly false. It advocates violation of the requirement for <u>objection</u> for <u>reason</u> <u>sustained</u> by the OPM (5 U.S.C. 3318(a)).

The DOJ actually argues <u>against</u> the requirement of <u>objection</u> and <u>reason</u> <u>sustained</u> by the OPM (5 U.S.C. 3318(a)), and <u>for</u> arbitrary nonhiring (5 U.S.C. 706 (2)(D)). It is fair to assume that DOJ attorneys comprehend 5 C.F.R. 731.101 and 5 U.S.C. 3318(a). Not only is their argument false, it is incredibly stupid.

IRS nonhiring that conceals "conviction," that omits suitability," that claims three <u>nonexistent</u> "considerations" as reason for nonhiring, is fraud--which the DOJ defends! Department of Justice? Rather, Department of Obfuscation (DOO).

The Selecting Officer's "failure to act" (5 U.S.C. 551(13)) invalidates every subsequent claim of lawful nonselection procedure. The DOJ, arguing for lawful nonselection, must argue deceptively. DOJ defense of the IRS has zero credibility.

# CHAPTER 7

# DECLARATION OF THE SELECTING OFFICER

I n support of their <u>Motion 04-4876</u>, defense counsel submitted to the Court the <u>DECLARATION OF LINDA G. SOTT</u>, Selecting Officer. The <u>DECLARATION</u> comprises fifteen <u>declarations</u> submitted under oath under penalty of perjury (18 U.S.C. 1621). Four <u>declarations</u> numbered 10, 11, 14, 15 deceive the Court. Yet, because it serves her evasion of review, Judge McLaughlin accepts them.

<u>Declaration 10</u>
The Agency made multiple selections under this certificate. For each selection, the Agency considered three applicants before making a selection and the Agency had the discretion to select anyone from among the three applicants.

Sott's claim of "considered three applicants" is a flat-out lie. "Three considerations" do not exist as confirmed by the FOIA search. "Discretion to select anyone" is discretion to select lower scoring in place of higher scoring applicants absent a reason--arbitrary selection--a violation of 5 U.S.C. 706(2)(A).

Lawful selection of a lower-scoring in place of a higher-scoring applicant requires objection to the higher scoring applicant for reason sustained by OPM (5 U.S.C. 3318(a)), notifying applicant, and his right to respond (5 C.F.R. 731.401-404). Absent the requirements, no law permits "discretion" to "select anyone."

If Sott had "discretion to select anyone," she could have selected me. After all, I had a high exam score, not determined unsuitable, yet not selected. Why not? Sott's concealed "conviction" not the reason? Failing to mention "conviction," Sott lies by omission, deceives. Declaration 10 is perjury, a felony (18 U.S.C. 1621).

### Declaration 11
Plaintiff was considered for three separate appointments, but other applicants were selected by the Agency.

A brazen lie. Again, three considerations do not exist, FOIA search confirmed the absence of any record of three considerations for appointment. I was not "considered" once, let alone thrice. Sott, noting "conviction" in the application failed to act (5 U.S.C. 551(13)), resulting in my immediate, unlawful removal from the competitive selection process, a violation of 5 U.S.C. 2302(b)(8)(A)(i).

Sott's term "considered" gives appearance of lawful procedure to the selection of "other applicants" with scores lower than mine absent OPM approval, which is unlawful. "Considered" means objection to applicant for reason sustained by the OPM--all omitted by Sott. Lying under oath is perjury, a felony (18 U.S.C. 1621).

### Declaration 14
For the third appointment to which Plaintiff was considered by the Agency, the Agency selected an applicant who had a rating of 90.0.

Three considerations do not exist. I was never "considered" for selection. Note Sott's failure to mention my higher score 90.6--a lie of omission. Selecting a lower scoring in place of a higher scoring applicant <u>not</u> sustained by OPM is fraud. Sott's term "considered" disguises as lawful her failure to select my higher 90.6 absent a reason for so doing. If she "considered," she would have <u>objected</u> for <u>reason sustained</u> by OPM prior to selecting the lower 90.0. Instead, fully aware of my higher score, she failed to act, a violation of 5 U.S.C. 2302(b)(8)(A)(i). The utter brazenness of Sott's lie reflects her belief that Judge McLaughlin accepts IRS violations.

Sott's omission of my score is the concealment of a material fact. Stating that I was "considered," she deceives by implying the existence of three nonexistent considerations. Concealing the material fact of my score is not "the truth, the whole truth, and nothing but the truth." Submitted to the Court under oath, <u>Declaration 14</u> is perjury, a felony (18 U.S.C. 1621). Habitual lying and deception, standard practice at the Directorate of Personnel Services--accepted by Judge McLaughlin.

Declaration 15

After the Agency considered Plaintiff for three appointments and he was not selected, plaintiff was not considered for any other appointments in accordance with 5 C.F.R. 332.405, an OPM regulation often referred to as the "rule of three.

Continuing the lie of three times considered, Sott claims the so-called "rule of three" (5 C.F.R. 332.405) as authority for non-hiring--absent <u>objection</u>, <u>reason, sustained</u> by OPM. Sott's lie under oath of three considerations is perjury. Four perjuries four felonies (18 U.S.C. 1621) accepted by a judge in cahoots with the IRS.

## Perjury defended

Employees in the Directorate of Personnel Services, the catch-bucket for habitual liars, lie easily, just part of the job. Every claim by IRS personnel to lawful procedure following Sott's "failure to act" is a lie defended by the DOJ. Did the DOJ verify Sott's DECLARATION? Maybe, maybe not. In either case, the DOJ defends Sott's perjury. The DOJ ("J" for "justice") trustworthy? A joke.

## Judge Giles dismissed without prejudice

Judge Giles did not accept defense counsel's arguments of "abuse of discretion" and failure "to state a claim." He accepted the argument of the "exhaustion of administrative remedies," it being a well-established doctrine. Accordingly, he dismissed without prejudice (04-4876) citing Muhammad v. Carlson,739 F.2D 122, 124, 3d Cir. 1984 (hereinafter Muhammad v. Carlson): "[t]he exhaustion doctrine does not preclude judicial relief, it simply postpones the timing of judicial adjudication." Also, citing Barnes v. Chatterton, 515 F.2d 916, (3d Cir., 1975, hereinafter Barnes v. Chatterton: "[t]he requirement that Barnes exhaust his administrative remedies thus affects only the timing, not the effectiveness of judicial review." The term "without prejudice" means the complaint, being undecided, is not barred, i.e., not precluded, from later review.

## CHAPTER 8

# ADMINISTRATIVE (MSPB) PROCESS INAPPLICABLE

### The MSPB lacks subject matter jurisdiction for review

Absent determination of unsuitability, the MSPB lacks subject matter jurisdiction to render a valid decision (5 C.F.R. 731.103(g)), (5 C.F.R 731.501(a)), (5 C.F.R. 1201.3(a)(7)). Moreover, an agency's "failure to select an applicant for the vacant position is generally not appealable to the Board" (Prewitt v. MSPB). Despite lack of MSPB jurisdiction, thus no right of MSPB appeal, Judge Giles's ruling that I exhaust administrative remedies requires appeal to the MSPB. Such "appeal," is contradictory, fruitless, planned by the IRS to result from Sott's "failure to act."

### Appealing to the nonjurisdictional MSPB

On date July 30, 2005 I submitted the "appeal" of IRS fraudulent nonhiring practice to the MSPB (Docket PH-0731-05-0545-I-1, November 28, 2005, hereinafter PH-0731). Because the MSPB lacks jurisdiction for review, the appeal is without substance, simply going through the motions, actually, a "so-called" appeal.

The so-called "appeal" is essentially the complaint filed at Court under 04-4876. It comprises the Selecting Officer's violations of lawful procedure:

1. "Failure to act," a violation of 5 U.S.C. 702
2. Selecting Officer's pretext of the nonexistence of "conviction," a violation of 5 U.S.C. 2302(b)(8)(A)(i)
3. Failure to pursue suitability, a violation of C.F.R. 731.101
4. Unlawful omission of suitability negates the right of MSPB appeal (5 C.F.R. 731.501(a))
5. Immediate removal of applicant from the field of competition absent <u>objection</u> and <u>reason</u> <u>sustained</u> by the OPM, a violation of 5 U.S.C. 3318(a)
6. The lie of the so-called "rule of three" (5 C.F.R. 332.405) as reason for "nonhiring" in <u>absence</u> of "three considerations"
7. Sott's deceptive concealment of "conviction," and my immediate removal from the selection process obstructed the right to compete for employment, a prohibited personnel practice, a violation of 5 U.S.C. 2302(b)(4)
8. "Simply non selecting" (IRM 6.331.1.20) is without observance of procedure required by law, a violation of 5 U.S.C. 706(2)(D)

MSPB dismissed for lack of jurisdiction

Administrative law Judge (ALJ) McStravick, on date November 28, 2005 dismissed the so-called "appeal" for lack of jurisdiction stating, "the instant matter is not within the Board's [MSPB's] jurisdiction as an employment practices appeal." (PH-0731, p. 11). The dismissal is based upon the following:

1a. The MSPB lacks jurisdiction over an agency's "failure to hire an applicant" and lacks authority to review an agency's procedures regarding selection or promotion (p. 3)
2a. There exists no right of appeal to the MSPB because"neither the IRS, nor the OPM made a suitability determination" (5 C.F.R. 731.501(a)) (p. 6)

3a. The MSPB lacks jurisdiction "in the absence of some law, rule, regulation or decision" that permits the appeal of an "unarticulated" or "constructive" [inferred] suitability determination by an applicant who "is not . . . at the present time, a tenured public employee" (pp.7, 8)

4a. The MSPB "has no jurisdiction to review" an agency's implementation or nonimplementation of "its own internal regulations" (p. 8)

5a. "[A]ssuming . . . the IRS acted improperly ["failure to act," "failure to <u>object</u> for proper <u>reason</u>, <u>sustained</u> by the OPM] in not selecting the appellant, I find the agency's use of the 'rule of three' against him was neutral in the sense that it became operative after he already had not [been] selected three times" (pp. 9, 10) ["neutral" means "rule of three" is irrelevant to the nonhiring]

6a. Regulation 5 C.F.R. 332.405 (falsely claimed by the IRS as cause of nonhiring), may only be reviewed by the MSPB Central Office, Washington, DC (Central Board)

(p.9)

### The so-called "appeal" to the Central Board

In order to complete the impossible task of exhausting nonexistent administrative remedies, a decision by the Central Board is required on the irrelevance of 5 C.F.R. 332.405. On date December 5, 2005, I submitted my nonadministrative, so-called "appeal" to the <u>nonjurisdictional</u> Central Board, a sterile process, as intended by the IRS with its failure to determine suitability.

Because the ALJ's dismissal for lack of jurisdiction is lawful (5 C.F.R. 731. 501(a)), "appealing" a lawful dismissal is contradictory. The "appeal" is simply to comply with the ALJ's comment regarding Central Board review of irrelevance of 5 C.F.R. 332.405 (and the duplicitousness of IRM 6.331.1.20). The "appeal," empty and time-consuming, delays the judicial review provided under 28 U.S.C. 1331.

The so-called "appeal" continues the charade of a <u>nonadministrative</u> complaint seeking a nonexistent <u>administrative</u> remedy. Absent determination of suitability, no law, rule, or regulation provides appellate jurisdiction to the MSPB/Central Board (5 C.F.R. 731.103(g); 731.501(a); 1201.3(a)(7)). Again, the chase after nonexistent administrative remedies plotted by the IRS to result from Sott's "failure to act"--which unlawfully <u>negates</u> the right of appeal to the MSPB.

The "appeal" to the MSPB's Central Board includes the following:

1b. Irrelevance of the "rule of three" (5 C.F.R. 332.405) claimed by Sott as <u>reason</u> for nonhiring, a ploy to mask her concealed "conviction" as <u>reason</u>

2b. Duplicity of IRM 6.331.1.20 which directs pursuit of suitability and simultaneously permits the IRS to "simply nonselect," <u>omitting</u> suitability, violating 5 C.F.R. 731.101

3b. Failure of the Selecting Officer to act on the "conviction" stated in the application, a violation of 5 U.S.C. 2302(b) (8) (A)(i)

4b. The so-called "rule of three" (5 C.F.R. 332.405) falsely claimed as reason for nonhiring, and my immediate removal from the field of competition obstructed by deception the right to compete for employment, a prohibited personnel practice (5 U.S.C. 2302(b)(4))

<u>Requires commission of prohibited personal practice?</u>
On date October 6, 2005, the Central Board denied review stating,

In sum, the petitioner has not shown that an OPM regulation on its face or as implemented by the IRS requires the commission of a prohibited personnel practice. Accordingly, the petitioner's regulation review is denied."

44

(Docket CB- 1205-06-0013-U-1, October 6, 2006, p. 8, hereinafter CB-1205.)

The ground for denial is absurd, a non sequitur to my complaint. I
had no intention of showing a regulation that "requires the commission of a prohibited personnel practice." A regulation that <u>requires</u>
the IRS to commit a prohibited personnel practice does not exist;
it is a Central Board fabrication. The Central Board "reviewed" its
fabrication and "ruled" on it, which illustrates the Central Board's
incapacity to decide a nonadministrative complaint for which the
APA provides Court, <u>not</u> MSPB/Central Board, jurisdiction (28
U.S.C. 1331).

### The Central Board's absurd, boilerplate response

The Central Board may respond only within the administrative
constraints imposed by regulation (5 C.F.R. 1201.3). Absent <u>un-
suitability</u>, the Central Board lacks jurisdiction over my claim.
Therefore, it responded with administrative boilerplate, i.e., failure to show a regulation that requires commission of a prohibited personnel practice. The response is absurd, the result of the
administrative (MSPB) process applied to my nonadministrative
complaint.

Because the Court, not the MSPB, is jurisdictional venue, the
doctrine of "exhaustion of administrative remedies" applied to a
nonadministrative complaint snarls the litigation. Sott's "failure to
act" omits suitability thus negates the MSPB's administrative appeals process. The doctrine, applied by Judge Giles as standard
procedure is a contradiction--intended by the IRS to be a wild-
goose chase.

### Central Board and requirement of a prohibited personnel practice

Central Board denial does not mean absence of a prohibited
personnel practice. Sott's deceptive "failure to act," her lie of

three "considerations," and my immediate removal from the selection process obstructed my right to compete for employment. Obstruction by deception of the right to compete is the very definition of prohibited personnel practice (5 U.S.C. 2302(b)(4))--and not required.

The blind-alley MSPB/Central Board appeal is the result of IRS unlawfully disregarding suitability, and Judge Giles's application of the doctrine of the "exhaustion of administrative remedies." Absent determination of unsuitability, the MSPB/Central Board lacks jurisdiction for review (5 C.F.R. 731.501(a)). The IRS's deceptive, unlawful policy of omitting suitability assures a sterile MSPB process.

### Authority for review: MSPB, no; Court, yes

Review of unlawful "failure to act" (5 U.S.C. 551(13)), defined by the APA as an "agency action," is not within MSPB venue for review. Pursuant to the APA, the Court is lawful venue for review (5 U.S.C. 702). Subject matter jurisdiction of the Court under 28 U.S.C. 1331.

# CHAPTER 9

# REFILING THE COMPLAINT

### Refiled complaint at Court, Civil Action 06-5325

Judge Giles's dismissal <u>without prejudice</u> (04-4876) permits refiling a claim at federal district court subsequent the "exhaustion of administrative remedies."

Because I was not determined unsuitable, and MSPB/Central Board lacking jurisdiction (5 C.F.R. 731.501(a)), I considered the irrational task of exhausting nonexistent administrative remedies completed. On date December 1, 2006, I refiled complaint of IRS deceptive, unlawful nonhiring practice at Court (<u>Muhammad v. Carlson; Barnes v. Chatterton</u>), Judge Mary A. McLaughlin presiding, the second judge assigned to this case (Civil Action 06-5325, hereinafter 06-5325).

### MSPB: may--not must--appeal to Fed. Cir

Judge McLaughlin responded, claiming the MSPB informed me that I "must" file any further appeal with the Fed. Cir. (06-5325, p.4). The MSPB however states, "may request Board" and Fed. Cir. "review this final [MSPB] decision," not that I "must" request their review (PH-0731, pp. 12, 13).

Procedure at 5 U.S.C. 7703 provides "the right to request the United States Court of Appeals for the Federal Circuit to review this final decision." It does not require the "right" to be exercised. It states, "applicant for employment adversely affected or aggrieved by a final order or decision of the Merit Systems Protection Board may obtain judicial review of the order or decision" (5 U.S.C. 7703(a)(1)).

"May obtain" does not mean "must obtain." Also, I was not "aggrieved" by the decision. I was bewildered by it. The Central Board's denial does not address my complaint, and is therefore irrelevant to it. Ground for appeal to the Fed. Cir. is the Central Board's denial based on its <u>fabrication</u> of my not showing an OPM regulation that requires the IRS's commission of a prohibited personnel practice. Appealing a fabricated requirement alien to my complaint is irrational. The Central Board is unscrupulous in fabricating an OPM "requirement" then passing off the fabrication as though it were the issue of my complaint.

The Central Board, an administrative venue, did not--could not lawfully--decide my nonadministrative "appeal" because it lacks the jurisdictional authority to do so. Significantly, the Central Board did <u>not</u> reverse the MSPB's dismissal for lack of jurisdiction. The issue of the IRS's deceptive, unlawful nonhiring practice is untouched by the Central Board's absurd denial, and remains undecided. The lawful venue for valid, final decision is Judge McLaughlin's Court with jurisdiction under 28 U.S.C. 1331, which she obsessively, unlawfully evades.

Because 5 U.S.C. 7703(a)(1) does not require Fed. Cir. review, and with Central Board denial based on a fabricated requirement, "appealing" the denial to the Fed. Cir. is as bizarre as the denial itself. The sterile chasing after nonexistent administrative remedies results from Sott's "failure to act," planned by the IRS to thwart an MSPB appeal against IRS deceptive, unlawful personnel practice.

### IRS motion to dismiss the refiling for lack of jurisdiction

Responding to the refiling, defense counsel, in the persons of the DOJ's Patrick L. Meehan, U.S. Attorney, and Virginia R. Powel, Assistant U.S. Attorney, on date March 7, 2007, submitted a Motion to Dismiss, (hereinafter Motion (06-5325) for lack of subject matter jurisdiction on grounds that I had not "appealed" the Central Board's denial to the Fed. Cir.

### Motion granted

Motion (06-5325) was granted by Judge McLaughlin. She dismissed on ground of lack of jurisdiction stating the Fed. Cir. has exclusive jurisdiction (06-5325, August 17, 2007, p. 6).

### Fed. Cir. "exclusive jurisdiction" and jurisdiction of the Court

"Exclusive jurisdiction" of the Fed. Cir. is part of the sterile, administrative appeals process forced upon my nonadministrative complaint by Judge Giles's application of the doctrine of the "exhaustion of administrative remedies." With Judge McLaughlin's dismissal, the charade of exhausting nonexistent remedies continues, but not without end. That is, "exclusive jurisdiction" of the Fed. Cir. is conditional and temporary. It is conditional upon the exhaustion of those nonexistent administrative remedies. It is temporary until the Fed. Cir. affirms the lack of MSPB jurisdiction which instantaneously ends the charade.

Review then reverts to the Court: "[a]gency action made reviewable by statute and final agency action for which there is no other adequate remedy in a court are [sic] subject to judicial review" (5 U.S.C. 704). The court "for which there is no other adequate remedy" is the Fed. Cir. The "final agency action" is, in fact, the initial "agency action," namely, Sott's "failure to act," for which the Court is assigned the duty of review (5 U.S.C. 702), jurisdiction under 28 U.S.C. 1331.

## A different judge acknowledges Court jurisdiction

Another judge, Judge Pratter, of the same district court in which Judge McLaughlin presides, in a case also concerning suitability, decided--contrary to Judge McLaughlin's deceptive denial of jurisdiction--"[t]he Court has federal question jurisdiction . . . under the Administrative Procedures Act pursuant to 28 U.S.C. 1331." Judge Pratter cited 5 U.S.C. 702 as providing judicial review: "a person suffering legal wrong because of an agency action . . . is entitled to judicial thereof." (Reginald Sydnor v. Office of Personnel Management, Civil Action No. 06-0014, 2007, hereinafter Sydnor v. OPM).

## The U.S. Court of Appeals for the Third Cir. affirms Court jurisdiction

The U.S. Court of Appeals for the Third Cir. held, "[t]he federal question statute, 28 U.S.C. 1331, provides the district courts with jurisdiction over all civil actions coming under the laws of the United States." (Fairview Township, County of York, Commonwealth of Pennsylvania v. United States Environmental Protection Agency, 73 F. 2d 517 (3d Cir. 1985). Judge McLaughlin ignores the precedent and refuses review of a lawful "cause of action" (254 A. 2d 824, 825).

## The U.S. Supreme Court affirms Court jurisdiction

The U.S. Supreme Court, with Pub. L. 94-574, 90 Stat. 2721 enacted by Congress October 21, 1976, stated 28 U.S.C. 1331 confers "jurisdiction on federal courts to review agency action." Califano v. Sanders, 430 U.S. 99, 105 (1977).

The U.S. Supreme Court held that, "if review is proper under the APA, the District Court had jurisdiction under 28 U.S.C. 1331." (Bowen v. Massachusetts, 487 U.S. 879, 891 n 16 (1988), hereinafter Bowen v. Massachusetts.)

The U. S. Supreme Court held that 5 U.S.C. 704 is the basis for "final agency action for which there is no other adequate remedy in a court" (Bennett v. Spear, 520 U.S. 154, 175 (1997), hereinafter Bennett v. Spear). Court jurisdiction subsequent Fed. Cir. decision is undeniable--ignored by Judge McLaughlin.

### Court, Third Cir., and U.S. Supreme Court affirm Court jurisdiction

Two Court judges, Judge Giles and Judge Pratter, acknowledge statute and precedent, and Court jurisdiction. U.S. Supreme Court, and Third Cir. affirm Court jurisdiction. Judge McLaughlin perversely ignores statute and precedent, denies Court jurisdiction, and dismisses on ground of lack of jurisdiction while simultaneously claiming ground of "issue preclusion"! The two grounds are contradictory, each unlawful, her dismissal an absolute fraud.

Ignoring the jurisdiction assigned her Court by U.S. Constitution, U.S. Supreme Court, and appellate court precedent, she dismisses fraudulently, by fiat, flouting Judge Giles's dismissal "without prejudice." Dismissal without prejudice means no final decision, which falsifies her claim of "issue preclusion."

### Nonselection a viable alternative to a formal determination?

Judge McLaughlin claims I argue IRM 6.331.1.20 provides "nonselection" as a viable alternative to a "formal" determination of suitability (06-5325, p. 6). "Viable alternative"? Alternative, yes. "Viable"--her word, not mine--no.

The Able Assistant, failing to attend to my claim, falsely advised Judge McLaughlin as to what I "argue." I "argue" that the wording of IRM 6.331.1.20 gives the Selecting Officer the choice of pursuing either lawful determination of suitability, or unlawful "simply non selecting" which erases suitability. IRM 6.331.1.20, provides a two-sided, self-contradictory process, therefore not "viable."

If the practice of "simply non selecting" were a "viable alternative," Sott, the Selecting Officer, would claim "simply non selecting" as lawful reason for nonhiring rather than claiming the lie of the so-called "rule of three" as reason. She made no such claim because "simply non selecting," which omits <u>objection</u> for <u>reason</u> <u>sustained</u> by OPM, violates 5 U.S.C. 3318(a) and reveals her unlawful "failure to act," as well she knows.

Sott, knowledgeable in suitability law and how to circumvent it, does not consider "simply non selecting" a viable alternative to a "formal" determination. Rather, she considers "simply non selecting" --which omits <u>objection</u> and <u>reason</u> <u>sustained</u> by the OPM--a viable ploy for <u>unlawfully omitting</u> suitability.

### "Viable alternative," Judge McLaughlin's creation

The term "viable alternative" does not originate with the Selecting Officer, or with the MSPB, or with me. It is the Able Assistant's and Judge McLaughlin's fabrication, their attempt to obscure the utter lawlessness of the IRS's practice of "simply nonselecting." It is their attempt to make the unlawful appear lawful.

Moreover, using the term "formal," Judge McLaughlin manipulates. She implies absence of the determination a minor deviation from lawful procedure. Suitability has no "formal" determination, only lawful determination. Absent lawful determination is nonexistent determination, a violation of 5 C.F.R. 731.101.

### Require prohibited personnel practice?

Judge McLaughlin argues that I "challenge" 5 C.F.R. 332.405 and IRM 6.331.1.20 on the basis that they <u>require</u> the performance of a prohibited personnel practice (06-5325, p.6), false argument.

I "challenge" Sott's claim of 5 C.F.R. 332.405 as <u>reason</u> for nonhiring--while she <u>conceals</u> "conviction" as reason! Concealed "conviction" fraudulently alters the critical content of the application. I claim IRM 6.331.1.20 provides the <u>choice</u> of lawfully determining suitability or unlawfully "simply non selecting," a violation of 5

U.S.C. 3318(a). "Choice" is opposite of "require." Sott chose "simply non selecting," while 332.405 requires nothing. I challenge Sott's use of 332.405 as cover for her lie of three implemented considerations that do not exist, a low IRS scam.

No OPM regulation requires a prohibited personnel practice. Judge McLaughlin repeats the Central Board's absurd denial (CB-1205) based on its fabricated "issue" of a regulation that requires the IRS's commission of a prohibited personnel practice, an "issue" that is not mine, that I did not raise, that doesn't exist.

Sott's deceptive, unlawful omission of the determination of suitability obstructed my right to compete for employment. The obstruction is a prohibited personnel practice (5 U.S.C. 2302(b)(4))--which is not required. The notion that a "prohibited personnel practice" occurs on condition of a law, rule, or regulation that requires such practice is arrant nonsense.

The so-called "rule of three" (5 C.F.R. 332.405), and IRM 6.331.1.20, each on its face or in its implementation, clearly do not require the commission of a prohibited personnel practice. If Judge McLaughlin believes I argue otherwise, she may provide a smidgeon of proof.

# CHAPTER 10

# REFILING OF COMPLAINT, A "DIRECT APPEAL"?

### Refiling at Court, an MSPB appeal?

Judge McLaughlin argues that refiling my complaint at Court--absent administrative (MSPB) remedies--is a direct appeal of the MSPB's lawful dismissal for lack of jurisdiction (06-5325, p.8). I do not appeal a lawful dismissal.

### Judge McLaughlin ignores MSPB lack of jurisdiction

Absent negative determination of suitability, the MSPB lacks jurisdiction over this case (5 C.F.R. 731.501(a)). Judge McLaughlin ignores my repeated statements of agreement with the MSPB's lawful dismissal on ground of lack of jurisdiction and perversely argues that I "appeal" the MSPB's lawful dismissal--this the unconscionable ploy of a district court judge who, by hook or by crook, seeks to evade review of a lawful cause of action. Evading review, she argues deceptively as "adjunct counsel for the defense," trashing law and judicial ethics in the process.

### "Appeal" to the unlikeliest forum

Moreover, had I disagreed with the MSPB's lawful dismissal, I should "appeal" to the Central Board not to the unlikeliest forum, the Court. Judge McLaughlin's "direct appeal" is false, as are all her arguments denying Court jurisdiction. Absent negative determination of suitability, Judge McLaughlin knows the MSPB lacks jurisdiction (5 C.F.R. 731.501(a)). Thus, the MSPB's dismissal is lawful. Arguing that I "appeal" the lawful dismissal, she attempts to deceive.

### Judge McLaughlin fabricates "direct appeal"

Claiming "direct appeal" of the MSPB's lawful dismissal for lack of jurisdiction, Judge McLaughlin seeks to force my nonadministrative complaint into the inapplicable administrative (MSPB) process where it comes to naught. No lawful authority exists for MSPB jurisdiction. Absent <u>unsuitability</u>, she cannot prove MSPB subject matter jurisdiction. She cannot truthfully deny jurisdiction of her Court affirmed under 28 U.S.C. 1331 and U.S. Supreme Court decision. She knows the MSPB lacks jurisdiction. Her phony "direct appeal" is nothing more than a ploy for evading review.

### Judge McLaughlin's claim of "direct appeal" is not credible

She is aware that statute (5 U.S.C. 702 and 704) and precedent (<u>Califano v. Sanders</u>; <u>Bowen v. Massachussetts</u>) provide <u>judicial</u>, not MSPB, review of wrongful agency action. She knows I claim lack of MSPB jurisdiction (5 C.F.R. 731.501(a)). Why would I "appeal" my own claim? Her argument is not credible. No language in the refiling is interpretable as an "appeal." Evading review, she deceives.

# CHAPTER 11

# JUDGE MCLAUGHLIN CREATES "INVISIBLE SUITABILITY"

<u>Existence of invisible determination of suitability?</u>
Judge McLaughlin will attempt--and fail--to prove the existence of "de facto" determination of suitability, i.e., existing in fact, but <u>invisible</u>. She supposes and attributes to me a claim that I was not selected for the reason of the IRS's having "made a negative suitability determination on the basis of his prior conviction" (06-5325, pp. 6, 7). She actually seeks to "prove" the <u>existence</u> of a negative--albeit <u>invisible</u>--determination, thus "proving" MSPB jurisdiction. What she proves is the desperate obsession of a judge scheming to evade review of a lawful cause of action.

<u>"Not selected," Judge McLaughlin's misleading term</u>
Applying the term "not selected" to an unlawful nonhiring, Judge McLaughlin misleads. Lawfully "not selected" requires <u>objection</u> to applicant for <u>reason</u> <u>sustained</u> by the OPM (5 U.S.C. 3318(a)). It also requires determination of suitability (5 C.F.R. 731.101), notification to applicant of his nonselection, and his right to respond (5 C.F.R. 731.402) all <u>omitted</u> by Sott with her "failure to act" (5 U.S.C. 551(13)). Therefore, I was not lawfully "not selected." Instead, with Sott's "failure to act," I was immediately, stealthily

dropped from the selection process, a silent fraud that obstructed the right to compete for employment--a prohibited personnel
practice (5 U.S.C. 2302(b)(4)).

## Lawful unsuitability and MSPB jurisdiction

Nonselection based on <u>unsuitability</u> provides MSPB jurisdiction
to review an appeal (5 C.F.R. 731.501(a)). If the MSPB decides applicant <u>unsuitable</u>, he may appeal to the Fed. Cir., whose decision,
positive or negative, concludes the complaint. Had Sott found me
unsuitable, my complaint would long ago have been resolved. It is
unresolved because, <u>absent</u> unsuitability, MSPB lacks jurisdiction,
and Judge McLaughlin unlawfully evades Court jurisdiction (28
U.S.C. 1331) and review.

## Judge McLaughlin claims that I argue the IRS made a suitability determination

Suitability determination does not exist. I argue the following:

1. Sott, failing to act (5 U.S.C. 551(13)), nullifies every subsequent personnel procedure the IRS claims as lawful
2. Sott, claiming the so-called "rule of three" as <u>reason</u> for
   nonhiring lies, knowing she omitted "three considerations"
3. Sott, noting "conviction" in the application, acted as though
   the application did not exist, a fraudulent personnel practice, a violation (18 U.S.C. 1001(c)(1))
4. "Conviction," derogatory information which requires determination of suitability (5 C.F.R. 731.202(b)(2), 5 U.S.C.
   2302(b)(8)(A)(i)), unlawfully <u>concealed</u> by Sott in order to
   avoid suitability determination
5. Sott stealthily dropped applicant from the selection process
   obstructed the right to compete for employment, a prohibited personnel practice (5 U.S.C. 2302(b)(4))
6. Sott, omitting OPM from the process, "adjudicated" a silent,
   in-her-psyche "determination" of <u>unsuitability</u>, a nonfact,

not discernible to the senses, a violation of lawful nonselection procedure (5 U.S.C. 3318(a))

7. No law, rule, or regulation authorizes silent, unwritten "adjudications" of negative suitability hatched in the psyches of Selecting Officers who unlawfully bypass OPM

8. If not "conviction" as <u>reason</u>, Sott's nonhiring is "arbitrary, capricious, an abuse of discretion, or otherwise not in accordance with law" (5 U.S.C. 706(2)(A))

9. I was granted a Presidential pardon based on a positive FBI background investigation, indicating an OPM investigation might also have been positive, cheated of it by Sott's unlawful omission of suitability

## Duty of the Court

Nonhiring, absent <u>objection</u> and <u>reason</u> <u>sustained</u> by the OPM, violates 5 U.S.C. 3318(a). The Selecting Officer's "failure to act" is a "legal wrong" for which the APA provides judicial review (5 U.S.C. 702). "Legal wrong" is ground for lawful cause of action (5 U.S.C. 704). Judge McLaughlin's duty is to review the complaint, which she evades by fraud disguised with legal-sounding verbiage.

Evading review, she claims IRS violations are lawful, an attempt to deceive. She claims issue preclusion as ground for dismissal--but in fact dismisses on ground of lack of jurisdiction, a blatant fraud (Civil Action 09-5941, hereinafter 09-5941). Absent <u>unsuitability</u>, Judge McLaughlin cannot prove MSPB jurisdiction (5 C.F.R. 731.501(a)), thus no right of MSPB appeal. The doctrine of equity is, "for every wrong, a remedy." Judge McLaughlin's "doctrine" is, "no remedy in Court for IRS unlawful nonhiring." This, despite remedy is in a Court with jurisdiction--her Court under 28 U.S.C. 1331 (<u>Bowen v. Massachusetts</u>, 487 U.S. 879, 891 n 16 (1988)) which she brazenly denies, violating Constitution and precedent.

# CHAPTER 12

# JUDGE MCLAUGHLIN CLAIMS FACTUAL SUITABILITY

<u>De facto (in fact) suitability determination "occurred"?</u>

B ased on advice of the Able Assistant, Judge McLaughlin, arguing as "adjunct counsel for the defense," claims that I argue a de facto suitability determination occurred, and that I request "review of that action" (06-5325, p. 8). To prove an APA violation, she argues that I must show "the IRS was required to make a determination, and that it failed to do so" (06-5325, p. 9, n 6).

Sott unlawfully bypassed OPM/FIPC, therefore no determination. Regarding occurrence of de facto determination, it does not simply "occur" as an act of nature, like rain--invisible no less! It must be <u>inferred</u> from a <u>discernible</u> agency action. The determination did not "occur" because Sott, the Selecting Officer, <u>intended</u> it to not "occur." With her "failure to act," Sott <u>insured</u> it did not "occur." No suitability determination or any lawful personnel procedure "occurs" following Sott's "failure to act." What "occurs" is Sott's concealment of "conviction" and outright lie of the "rule of three" as reason for nonhiring. I argue it is the <u>IRS</u> "must show" the reason for nonhiring, and the reason for the absence of the determination of suitability the IRS stated in its ESNA <u>would</u> be processed.

## I must "show" the requirement for suitability?

Judge McLaughlin does not need me to "show" a requirement for the IRS to determine suitability. It is "shown" at 5 C.F.R. 731.101 which states, "pursuant to 5 U.S.C. 3301 and E.O. [Executive Order] 10577, Section 3301of title 5, United States Code, directs . . . OPM to examine suitability for competitive Federal employment." "Directs" means <u>required</u>--do it! The examination did not "occur" because Sott unlawfully omitted OPM from the process. A stated conviction in the application requires suitability be examined by OPM/FIPC investigation. In order to avoid suitability, Sott chose to ignore lawful procedure. With her "failure to act," she <u>concealed</u> the conviction, a stealthy IRS scam for avoiding suitability. She failed to <u>object</u>, failed to provide a <u>reason</u> for nonhiring, and failed to refer the nonhiring to OPM in violation of 5 U.S.C. 3318(a). Judge McLaughlin, evading review unethically, deceptively defends Sott's violations.

Queried for the reason for nonhiring, IRS employees respond with the standard lie of "rule of three" as reason. They profit from immediate removal of applicant because it is "efficient, which leads to "quality salary increase," standard, corrupt practice at the IRS Directorate of Personnel Services.

## Judge McLaughlin aware of MSPB lack of jurisdiction (5 C.F.R. 731.501(a))

Judge McLaughlin is aware the MSPB lacks jurisdiction, (06-5325, August 17, 2007, p. 8). Lacking jurisdiction, the MSPB dismissal is lawful (5 C.F.R. 731.501(a)). Yet, so obsessed is she to evade the jurisdiction of her Court, she attempts to prove existence of nonexistent MSPB jurisdiction.

## De facto suitability, Judge McLaughlin's false argument

Judge McLaughlin claims I argue for de facto suitability, that I request "review of that action" (06-5325, p. 8). Yet there was no action. I argue Sott <u>failed</u> to act, omitting <u>objection</u>, <u>reason</u>, <u>suitability</u>, and

OPM review in violation of 5 U.S.C. 3318(a), and 5 C.F.R. 731.101. I argue venue for review of "failure to act" is Judge McLaughlin's Court (5 U.S.C. 702), jurisdiction under 28 U.S.C. 1331.

## Suitability determination, not mandated?

Judge McLaughlin argues that former employees may request determination of suitability under 5 C.F.R. 731.601 (Sydnor v. OPM). She argues, "[n]o such language mandates that an agency make a negative determination before appointment" (06-5325, p. 9, n 6)--incredible. Negative determination not required means every applicant would be suitable. Also, Sydnor concerns determination of unsuitability. I was not determined unsuitable. Sydnor is inapplicable to my case.

The "determination before appointment" to which she refers is, in fact, a redetermination following the initial determination (5 C.F.R. 731.601(a)). Because Sott failed to act (5 U.S.C. 551(13)), there is no initial determination. I do not claim redetermination of suitability. I claim Sott's concealment of "conviction," a stealthy revision of my application--forgery--a ploy for erasing suitability.

If, as Judge McLaughlin claims, negative determination is not mandated, any applicant, no matter his background, may be selected at whim of the Selecting Officer. To avoid such dysfunction, suitability of every applicant must be determined 5 C.F.R. 731.101). Applicants for GS-04, low-level clerical positions are selected when their background evinces no derogatory information. I stated derogatory information, i.e., "conviction," in the application, which requires suitability as stated in the ESNA, repeated at IRM 10.23.3.1, omitted by Sott. Judge McLaughlin's argument for nonmandatory suitability is false. Any argument to evade review.

## Judge McLaughlin defends IRS fraud

Judge McLaughlin, aware of 5 C.F.R. 731.101, is aware that every applicant must be determined suitable for the job for which he applied. She is aware that Sott's "failure to act" is the failure to take a personnel action (5 U.S.C. 2302(b) (8)(A)(i)), which is the fraudulent concealment of the stated "conviction." She is aware that "failure to act" is an actionable wrong (5 U.S.C. 702). Yet, to evade review, she defends Sott's "failure to act," fraudulent concealment of "conviction," and unlawful omission of suitability. Evading review, she accepts the lie of the "rule of three" as reason for nonhiring, ignoring "conviction" as reason. This, the sheer hypocrisy of a judge of the federal district court.

Sott's "failure to act," i.e., concealment of the conviction (18 U.S.C. 1001(a)(1)), is a silent, stealthy "alteration" of my application from one that states "conviction" to one that doesn't. It is appalling that Sott's violation of law is defended by a judge of the federal district court who subverts law in order to evade her Court's jurisdiction thereby evading her duty of review.

### "May take suitability action," a matter of agency choice?

On advice of the Able Assistant, Judge McLaughlin, arguing as "adjunct counsel for the defense," citing 5 C.F.R. 731.105(b), states, "an agency may take suitability action, not that it must" (06-5325, p. 9, n 6). She falsely refers to the determination itself as a "suitability action." First is the determination. The "suitability action" follows the determination. If the determination is negative, the "suitability action" is nonselection. If determination is positive, the "suitability action" is selection.

Suitability is basic to federal employment. Suitability for the job sought is <u>required</u> of every applicant to the competitive service (5 C.F.R. 731.101). Her "may take" argument is false. Agencies <u>must</u> take action. Absence of suitability negates MSPB jurisdiction (5 C.F.R. 731.501(a)). "Failure to act," a nonaction, is for Court review (5 U.S.C. 702). Defending the IRS with her "may take" argument, Judge McLaughlin, in effect, argues for arbitrary determination (5 U.S.C. 706(2)(A)). Evading review, she subverts law.

<u>Enumerated list of factors (5 C.F.R. 731.202(b)) not necessary?</u>
Judge McLaughlin, citing 5 C.F.R. 731.202(b) argues, "the enumerated list of factors 'may' be considered a basis for determinations" of
suitability (06-5325, p. 9, n 6). If factors <u>may</u> be considered, they also
<u>may not</u> be considered, with every applicant selected, absent determi-
nation. She argues the list of factors are irrelevant for selection, thus
advocating arbitrary selection. She fails, however, to state the "basis
for [negative] determinations" if the factors are not considered.

She ignores 5 C.F.R. 731.202(a) which states, "an agency . . .
shall make its determination on the basis of the specific factors in
paragraph (b) of this section." The term "shall" overpowers Judge
McLaughlin's "may." Ignoring the list of factors, she ignores 5
C.F.R. 731.202(a) and defends nonhiring at whim of the Selecting
Officer, a practice "arbitrary, capricious . . . not in accordance with
law" (5 U.S.C. 706(2)(A)).

Judge McLaughlin's arguments in defense of IRS unlawful
nonhiring are untenable. She cannot validly defend Sott's unlawful "failure to act" (5 U.S.C. 2302(b)(8) (A)(i)) which prevents subsequent, lawful personnel procedure.

No actionable claim?
Based on the Able Assistant's advice, namely, "an agency may take
suitability action, not that it must," Judge McLaughlin argues that
I do "not have an actionable claim" (06-5325, p. 9, n 6). Sott's "failure to act," not actionable?

Judge McLaughlin's "not actionable" argument, is false. Sott's
"failure to act" is defined as an "agency action" (5 U.S.C. 551(13)),
judicially reviewable (5 U.S.C. 702). Moreover, a "reviewing court
shall compel agency action [compel determination of suitability] unlawfully withheld . . . [5 U.S.C. 706(1)], and hold unlawful and set
aside agency action, findings, and conclusions" found unlawful (5
U.S.C. 706(2)(A)-(D)). Not actionable? On the contrary, absolutely
actionable.

Sott's "failure to act" is the fraudulent concealment of "conviction" and omission of suitability. It is the deception that underlies the immediate, unlawful dropping applicant from the selection process. So doing, she obstructs his right to compete for employment, a prohibited personnel practice (5 U.S.C. 2302(b)(4)). Sott's "failure to act" is what Judge McLaughlin, acting as "adjunct counsel for the defense," defends. This is a federal judge defending IRS violation of law.

Suitability, derogatory information, and enumerated factors
Evading review, Judge McLaughlin defends IRS violation of OPM procedure IRM 10.23.3.1: "[s]uitability determinations must [emphasis added] be made when derogatory information about an applicant or employee surfaces in the course of pre-employment or background investigations." The word "must" permits no omission of the determination. IRM 10.23.3.1 requires ". . . potential employees undergo" suitability investigations.

The stated conviction, an "enumerated factor," is derogatory information which requires determination of suitability. Sott, however, failed to act (5 U.S.C. 551(13)), ignored enumerated factors, and omitted the determination in violation of 5 C.F.R. 731.101; these violations Judge McLaughlin cynically "legitimizes."

"Enumerated factors" are essential to "the efficiency of the service" (5 C.F.R. 731.202(a)). Judge McLaughlin, arguing the IRS may consider the factors, argues against their necessity and for arbitrary selection. Arguing the factors are unnecessary, she argues for undermining "the efficiency of the service," an untenable argument. She resorts to any argument, even one obviously false, to evade review.

No final judgment (06-5325), no resolution of my claim
Judge McLaughlin dismissed for of lack of jurisdiction (06-5325), therefore she rendered no judgment of unsuitability. Absent

determination of unsuitability, the MSPB lacks jurisdiction to render a valid decision (5 C.F.R. 731.501(a)). My complaint, forced into the administrative (MSPB) process of the "exhaustion of administrative remedies," is therefore in a sterile process, meaning no MSPB resolution. The sterile process continues with appeal to the Fed. Cir.

## Subsequent Fed. Cir. appeal, Court jurisdiction may not be denied

Subsequent Fed. Cir. appeal, reality kicks in with the Fed. Cir. affirming MSPB lack of jurisdiction. Fed. Cir. affirmation discredits Judge McLaughlin's claim of MSPB jurisdiction. The forced charade of exhausting nonexistent, administrative remedies ends, and her Court with jurisdiction under 28 U.S.C. 1331, which she unscrupulously denies, emerges from the swamp of her deceptions as the undeniable, jurisdictional venue for review (Muhammad v. Carlson; Barnes v. Chatterton).

# CHAPTER 13

# DOJ: DIRECT APPEAL-MERITS OF SUITABILITY-RULE OF THREE

### Defense counsel's hodgepodge: "direct appeal, merits of suitability, rule of three"

In Motion 06-5325 (p. 8), the DOJ argues that my refiling "is a direct appeal [another one?] of both the ALJ's decision on the merits of suitability and the MSPB's final decision upholding the validity of OPM 'rule of three' regulation must be dismissed for lack of subject matter jurisdiction." The argument, a hodgepodge of confused, obfuscating verbiage is the DOJ's pathetic defense.

### "Direct appeal," a defense counsel fabrication

The MSPB states, "in the absence of some law, rule, regulation, or decision permitting Board review of whether agency selection actions were based on unarticulated or non-formal suitability determinations, that there is no basis for accepting this appeal as within the Board's jurisdiction." (PH-0731, pp.7, 8). Absent suitability, the MSPB lacks jurisdiction for review (5 C.F.R. 731.103(g); 731. 501(a); 1201.3(a)(7)). Refiling the complaint is not an appeal, direct or indirect. It is the continuation of the complaint at Court for which the Court, not the MSPB, has subject matter jurisdiction for review (28 U.S.C. 1331).

The DOJ's "direct appeal" is a fabrication. It obscures both the IRS's unlawful omission of suitability and the jurisdiction of the Court. The DOJ seeks to entangle the claim in the dead-end, administrative (MSPB) appeals process, abetted by Judge McLaughlin who evades review by defending IRS violations.

### Defense counsel's obfuscation: "merits of suitability"

The DOJ creates the oxymoron "merits of suitability" and attributes it to the ALJ, who made no comment construable as "merits of suitability." Linking merits and suitability, the DOJ obfuscates. "Merits" refers solely to the substance of the issues of my complaint, e.g., Sott's unlawful "failure to act," concealment of "conviction," and lie of "three considerations." Issues have merits. "Suitability" has no "merits." Suitability is a requirement underlying lawful selection procedure.

"Suitability" refers to whether "an individual's character or conduct may have an impact on the integrity or efficiency of the service" (5 C.F.R. 731.202(a)). The requirement for suitability exists independent of issues of IRS deceptive, unlawful nonhiring. Sott, ignoring the requirement, is defended by Director, Richard J. Cronin, by the DOJ, and by Judge McLaughlin who evades review of a lawful cause of action. The "public servants," namely, IRS, DOJ, and Judge McLaughlin betray public trust and defend the IRS's corrupt circumvention of suitability.

The DOJ's jumbled "merits of suitability" blurs the ALJ's lawful dismissal. Jumbled verbiage is a DOJ tactic of deception. It attests to the impossibility of the DOJ's forming a valid defense of IRS blatant violations of law. The DOJ defends IRS's unlawful omission of suitability by obscuring it.

## Upholding validity of OPM "rule of three" regulation, and "final decision"

The DOJ argues that the MSPB upheld "the validity of OPM 'rule of three' regulation," an argument that implies the "rule of three" as lawful reason for nonhiring. The continual reference to "rule of three" is the attempt to deceive. The DOJ's claim of "three considerations" is a lie; three considerations do not exist.

Moreover, the ALJ states, "the agency's use of the 'rule of three' against him was neutral in the sense that it became operative after he already had not [been] selected three times" (PH-0731, pp. 10, 11). The "rule," invoked after nonhiring, is therefore irrelevant to the nonhiring. Thus, the ALJ reveals the IRS's and DOJ's claim of the "rule of three" as prior reason for nonhiring as the lie that it is.

The DOJ claims MSPB "final decision" while referring to "validity," an attempt to deceive. The MSPB dismissed for lack of jurisdiction, meaning absence of valid "final decision." Craftily intermixing the terms "final decision" and "validity," the DOJ fabricates an MSPB "valid final decision," a DOD deception. Only by obfuscating and deceiving do DOJ attorneys defend the IRS's deceptive, unlawful employment practice. DOJ attorneys are as crooked as their client IRS.

## Issues not reviewed for lack of MSPB jurisdiction remain unresolved

The overriding issue is the IRS's violation of law, e.g., "failure to act" (5 U.S.C. 551(13)); failure to pursue suitability (5 C.F.R. 731.101), failure to object for proper reason sustained by the OPM (5 U.S.C. 3318(a)), failure "to take . . . a personnel action [i.e. determination of suitability] (5 U.S.C.2302 (b)(8)(A)(i)), immediate dropping of applicant from the field of competition obstructing his right to compete for employment, a prohibited personnel practice (5 U.S.C. 2302(b)(4)), Sott's perjurious Declarations to the Court, a felony (18 U.S.C. 1621).

IRS violations of law are subject to Court, not MSPB, review. The violations are a lawful "cause of action" (5 U.S.C. 704, see Califano v. Sanders). Absent Court review under 28 U.S.C. 1331, issues remain unresolved.

### Sott's claim of the "rule of three" not credible

Sott, noting "conviction" in the application fails to act, immediately drops applicant from consideration, then claims the so called "rule of three" as reason for nonhiring. Her noting "conviction" precedes her claim of "rule of three," as reason. "Conviction" is therefore the actual reason for nonhiring. Claiming the "rule of three" as reason while not implementing three considerations, Sott lies.

### The trap of the administrative (MSPB) appeals process

The administrative (MSPB) process applied to a nonadministrative complaint has tied this case in knots. Applicants and attorneys must forestall the dead-end litigation of a nonadministrative claim forced into the administrative process of exhausting nonexistent, administrative remedies. The Court, not the MSPB, has jurisdiction over IRS violations, e.g., "failure to act" (5 U.S.C. 702).

### Applicants must verify existence of "three considerations"

Applicants for employment not selected, not notified, and later learn the reason for nonhiring is the "rule of three," must verify an existent record of three implemented considerations. Absent record, the IRS defrauds applicants of suitability and possible employment, as in the following Lackhouse cases.

# CHAPTER 14

# LACKHOUSE DECISION, RULE OF THREE, FED. CIR. ERROR

### The Lackhouse cases and IRS fraud of the "rule of three"

In response to the query for the <u>reason</u> for nonhiring, IRS employees claim the "rule of three" as reason, a lie knowing three considerations do not exist. In prior cases they have gotten away with their deceptive, unlawful nonhiring by claiming "rule of three" as reason. This is illustrated in a complaint against the IRS brought before the Fed. Cir.: <u>Raymond G. Lackhouse v. Merit Systems Protection Board</u>, 734 F.2d 1471 (Appeal No. 83-896, Fed. Cir., 1984), and 773 F. 2d 313 (Appeal No. 85-2141, 1985).

Mr. Lackhouse, a former veteran, therefore a "preference eligible" with <u>right</u> of MSPB appeal, was "passed over," meaning nonhired. He was not notified, a violation of 5 U.S.C. 3317(b) and 3318(b). He did not learn of the pass-over until July 27, 1981 when he contacted the IRS (734 F. 2d 1471, p. 1). Mr. Lackhouse appealed the pass-over to the MSPB. The MSPB dismissed for lack of jurisdiction.

### Absence of reason for Mr. Lackhouse's "nonselection"

He then appealed to the Fed. Cir. which remanded to the MSPB to examine "possible procedural errors surrounding Lackhouse's nonselection" (734 F. 2d 1471, p. 1). "Possible procedural errors" is the crux of the remand, specifically the "error" of the <u>absence</u> of <u>reason</u> for the "nonselection." The MSPB again dismissed for lack of jurisdiction. Again, Mr. Lackhouse appealed to the Fed. Cir.

The case was then reviewed by three different Fed. Cir. judges. Contrary to the crux of the remand, the three judges did <u>not</u> examine "possible procedural errors," specifically the "error" of the <u>absence</u> of the reason for three pass-overs. Instead, relying on IRS explanation of "rule of three," they considered whether the "rule of three" was validly or invalidly applied (773 F. 2d 313, p.1). If validly applied, Mr. Lackhouse was lawfully passed over.

### IRS explanation: spreadsheet/three considerations

The IRS explained that a "spreadsheet" was prepared listing applicants in rank order, then making selections from the top three applicants in sequential order of their place on the list (773 F. 2d 313, p. 2). Accepting the explanation on its face, the three judges stated, "IRS also utilized <u>5 C.F.R. 332.405</u> (the 'rule of three'), permitting an appointing officer to drop from consideration" an applicant not selected after three considerations. The spreadsheet itself does not refer to "three considerations" or to the reason for Mr. Lackhouse's pass-over. The IRS merely <u>implies</u> 5 C.F.R. 332.405 as reason. The judges, failing to examine <u>absence</u> of <u>rea</u>son for three pass-overs, <u>assumed</u> the "three considerations" included the reason.

The "spreadsheet" provides no evidence of OPM <u>sustaining</u> a <u>reason</u> for the pass-overs. Absence of both <u>reason</u> and OPM from the process violates 5 U.S.C. 3318(a) and invalidates the judges' assumption that the "IRS also utilized <u>5 C.F.R. 332.405</u>" as being lawful reason for dropping Mr. Lackhouse from consideration. No record of "three considerations" were evidenced. The IRS, implying their existence, hoodwinked the three judges. The "spreadsheet" itself is irrelevant as <u>reason</u> for the pass-over. To the detriment of Mr. Lackhouse, the three judges swallowed the IRS's phony "spreadsheet" explanation hook, line, and sinker.

Accepting without question the "spreadsheet" explanation, and <u>assuming</u> the existence of "three considerations," is the error in the three judges' decision. They were duped by the IRS into believing the existence of three nonexistent considerations. Thus, implementing the deceptive "rule of three" swindle, the IRS successfully defended its fraudulent pass-over of Mr. Lackhouse.

Failing to examine the reason for the pass-over, instead accepting the phony "spreadsheet" explanation, the three judges denied Mr. Lackhouse due process, namely, IRS implementation of three "considerations," <u>reason</u> for the pass-over sustained by the OPM, and notifying him of his decertification (5 U.S.C. 3317(b)).

### <u>Standard practice: IRS deceptive, unlawful nonhiring</u>
The <u>Lackhouse</u> cases reveal the IRS's deceptive, unlawful nonhiring practice, covered up by the "rule of three," as standard practice existing at least since 1981.

# CHAPTER 15

# ABSENT APPEAL TO FED. CIR., COMPLAINT VALID

### Validity of complaint

The absence of appeal to the Fed. Cir. and dismissal of my complaint for lack of jurisdiction (06-5325) do not affect the validity of the complaint. The IRS's violations remain, as does jurisdiction of the Court subsequent the "exhaustion of administrative remedies" (Muhammad v. Carlson; Barnes v. Chatterton).

### Corrective to the absence of Fed. Cir. appeal

Corrective to the absence of Fed. Cir. appeal is to appeal the MSPB's lawful dismissal for lack of jurisdiction to the Fed. Cir.-- notwithstanding the irrationality of appealing a lawful dismissal. Absent negative determination of suitability, the MSPB's dismissal is lawful (5 C.F.R. 731.501(a)).

### "Appealing" a lawful dismissal, a contradictory, sterile process

Appealing a lawful MSPB dismissal to the Fed. Cir. is a dead-end, contradictory process, the result of applying the administrative doctrine of the "exhaustion of administrative remedies" to a nonadministrative complaint. The lawful venue for the complaint of "failure to act" (5 U.S.C. 702) is the federal district court, Judge McLaughlin's Court (28 U.S.C. 1331).

## The DOJ obfuscates the complaint

While defense counsel DOJ obfuscates with the oxymoronic "merits of suitability," there is no obfuscating the facts of the Selecting Officer's violations: "failure to act" (5 U.S.C. 551(13)), omission of "suitability" (5 C.F.R. 731.101), fraudulent personnel practice of concealment of "conviction" (18 U.S.C. 1001(a)(1), failure to take a personnel action regarding "conviction" (5 U.S.C. 2302(b)(8)(A)(i)), obstruction by deception of the right to compete for employment a prohibited personnel practice (5 U.S.C. 2302(b)(4)), lying under oath of implementing "three considerations" that were not implemented--perjury a felony (18 U.S.C. 1621).

DOJ attorneys cannot validly defend the IRS's chain of violations. Thus, they obscure Court jurisdiction with double-talk such as "merits of suitability," attempting to throw the complaint to the MSPB, where it comes to naught.

Had "three considerations" comprising <u>objection</u>, <u>reason</u>, <u>sustained</u> by the OPM been implemented (5 U.S.C. 3318(a)) instead of Sott's "failure to act" (5 U.S.C. 551(13)), and were I determined unsuitable, my complaint would be within the administrative (MSPB) appeals process (5 C.F.R. 731.501(a)); absent the determination, it is not. Lawful venue for IRS "failure to act" is the Court (5 U.S.C. 702), jurisdiction under 28 U.S.C. 1331.

# CHAPTER 16

# COURT JURISDICTION, JUDICIAL BIAS, AND IRM 6.331.1.20

### Court jurisdiction, not MSPB jurisdiction

E vading review, Judge McLaughlin obsessively attempts to sell the bogus notion of MSPB jurisdiction, despite 28 U.S.C. 1331 which provides judicial, not MSPB jurisdiction for IRS violations. Because her Court has jurisdiction she evades review by fiat dismissals on false ground of lack of jurisdiction.

### Judge McLaughlin's fiction of "certain procedures"

Based on the Able Assistant's research, Judge McLaughlin states requirements for lawful nonselection: (1) "negative suitability determinations" based on "criminal history" (5 C.F.R. 731.202), and (2) "an agency must follow certain procedures, including providing notice of the decision and opportunity to challenge the finding" (06-5325, p. 7). She argues that I allege my "non-selection" was due to "the prior conviction, but absent these certain procedures" (06-5325, p. 7). She deceptively uses the term "non-selection," a lawful procedure, to mask IRS unlawful nonhiring.

I do not allege absence of "certain procedures," Judge McLaughlin's misleading term. I allege violation of <u>lawful</u> procedures. Sott's "failure to act," concealed "conviction," omission of "suitability," and lie of "three considerations" are not the absence of "certain procedures." They are violations of law. Judge McLaughlin's term "certain procedures" obscures Sott's violations. Using the term "non-selection," she implies Sott's immediate, unlawful dropping of applicant is lawful, a deception as she ignores Sott's concealment of "conviction." With Sott's "failure to act," I was immediately dropped from consideration (5 U.S.C. 702). I should have no complaint were I lawfully nonselected based on determination of unsuitability with right of MSPB appeal. Evading jurisdiction and review, Judge McLaughlin whitewashes the IRS's violations, abetting and protecting the IRS.

Because Sott failed to act (5 U.S.C. 551(13)), Judge McLaughlin knows suitability is not determined, thus no "notice of the decision," and no "opportunity to challenge the finding." Yet, despite absence of suitability, she attempts to prove its existence, resorting to deception to do so, an irrational, obsessive behavior.

### Judge McLaughlin unethically, unlawfully biased in favor of the IRS

Judge McLaughlin, referring to the absence of "certain procedures," obscures Sott's violations of lawful procedures. To evade review of a lawful "cause of action" (5 U.S.C. 704), she argues as "adjunct counsel for the defense," exhibiting a deceptive, unethical judicial bias in favor of the IRS.

### IRM 6.331.1.20, rationale for unlawful nonhiring

Sott, the Selecting officer, whose ready violation of law demonstrates she may do so with impunity fails to act, thus conceals the application's stated conviction. The concealment alters the critical content of the application. That is, by concealing "conviction," she virtually "rewrites"--falsifies--the application, a virtual forgery. The concealment covers up her fraudulent omission of suitability and the immediate, unlawful dropping of applicant from the competitive selection process, a prohibited personnel practice (5 U.S.C. 2302(b)(4)).

Then, pursuant to IRM 6.331.1.20, she proceeds with the fraudulent practice of nonhiring, that is, "simply 'non selecting' and working within the 'rule-of-three' for consideration." Simply non selecting is, in fact, the "failure to act." The phrase "working within the 'rule-of-three' for consideration" provides rationale for her deceptive claim of "three considerations" as reason for nonhiring, obscuring "conviction" as reason. Three considerations do not exist. Claiming their existence, Sott lies, standard practice at the Directorate of Personnel Services. In order to evade review, Judge McLaughlin without scruple embraces Sott's lie.

It is understandable that Sott acts as though she has the right to falsify an application. In the self-serving, mendacious culture of the IRS's Directorate of Personnel Services, where deceptive, unlawful omission of suitability is standard practice defended by Director, Richard J. Cronin, she has that right. Cronin is essential to the practice.

The IRS, able to violate law with impunity--while it has punitive power over the public--is a direct threat to the personal security of every one of us. Judge McLaughlin, defending instead of reviewing IRS violations, is complicit in IRS violations. As such, she exposes every one of us to wrongful IRS action.

# CHAPTER 17

# "DE FACTO" SUITABILITY AND MSPB JURISDICTION, PROVED?

### "De facto" suitability gives MSPB jurisdiction

On advice of the Able Assistant, Judge McLaughlin attempts to prove de facto suitability, i.e., existing in fact but invisible. But why invisible when "conviction," stated in the application--unlawfully concealed by Sott--virtually screams "suitability"? Answer: invisible suitability, if proved, provides MSPB jurisdiction, by which she evades review. Invisible suitability is the cynical ploy of a judge aware of Sott's "failure to act," which <u>concealed</u> the stated conviction. What she proves is judicial chicanery in order to evade review.

### "De facto" suitability impossible

Judge McLaughlin's de facto suitability is invisible because it doesn't exist. No lawful procedure exists following Sott's "failure to act" (5 U.S.C. 551(13)). What exists is Sott's lie of the "rule of three" as reason for nonhiring. De facto suitability is Judge McLaughlin's con game. Existent suitability, the creation of existence from nonexistence, Judge McLaughlin's divine miracle? Not likely.

<u>Sott's psychical determination and "adjudication" of suitability</u>
Sott, noting "conviction" in the application ignored the requirement for OPM/FIPC examination of suitability. Instead, she "adjudicated" a silent, invisible determination of suitability hatched in
her psyche. No law, rule, or regulation authorizes silent, invisible
determinations hatched in the psyches of Selecting Officers. The
OPM, not Sott, lawfully adjudicates suitability--<u>visible</u>, written suitability. Sott, failing to act, bypassed OPM and stealthily dropped
applicant from the selection process--meaning no determination.
By fraud, she obstructed his right to compete for employment, a
prohibited personnel practice (5 U.S.C. 2302(b)(4)).

<u>Absent determination, absent MSPB jurisdiction</u>
Because I am not a federal employee, the MSPB lacks jurisdiction
absent a negative determination of suitability (5 C.F.R. 731.501(a)).
The criteria for negative determinations are stated at 5 C.F.R.
731.202. Sott's "failure to act" concealed the criterion of "conviction," omitted suitability, and thereby "erased" MSPB jurisdiction. Because "failure to act," an IRS wrong, is to be reviewed
by the Court under 5 U.S.C. 702, the U.S. Supreme Court affirmed district court jurisdiction under 28 U.S.C. 1331 (<u>Bowen
v. Massachussetts</u>). Absent negative determination, the MSPB has
no part in IRS unlawful nonhiring. Ignoring Supreme Court, statute, and precedent Judge McLaughlin evades jurisdiction unlawfully, and dismisses by fiat on false ground of lack of jurisdiction.

<u>IRS reason for nonhiring remains unknown</u>
Owing to Sott's "failure to act" (5 U.S.C. 551(13)), the actual reason
for the nonhiring remains unknown. My claim of "conviction" as
reason is merely a guess. There may be a different reason also concealed. Because of her "failure to act," Sott's reason for nonhiring

is not discernible. Perhaps she decided to simply not select, an unwitting violation of 5 U.S.C. 706(2)(A). Perhaps she thought the fraudulent, omission of suitability is not fraudulent. Perhaps she believes "failure to act," omitting FIPC adjudication by the OPM, is time-saving, efficient, therefore standard practice. Perhaps any reason, except the obvious reason staring her in the face, namely, "conviction," which she deceptively, unlawfully concealed.

### "Constructing" a suitability determination

Advised by the Able Assistant, Judge McLaughlin argues that the "MSPB has dealt with claims of this nature," i.e., unrecorded determinations of suitability. She states, "[r]ather than classify them as claims for failure to follow procedures, it has referred to them as claims for 'de facto' or 'constructive' suitability determinations" (06-5325, p. 7). De facto suitability may indeed be "constructed," not from schemes percolating in Sott's psyche, but from perceivable fact.

### Suitability inferred from a verifiable agency action

Thus de facto determination may be <u>inferred</u> from a verifiable agency <u>action,</u> a fact discernible to the senses. If Judge McLaughlin can prove such agency action--in face of Sott's "failure to act"--de facto determination may be "constructed." Jurisdiction is then with the MSPB, not with the Court. Because Sott failed to act, agency action discernible to the senses is, in fact, nonexistent.

The IRS intended to negate MSPB appeal of its deceptive, unlawful nonhiring practice, and did so with Sott's "failure to act," which "erases" both suitability and right of MSPB appeal (5 C.F.R. 731.501(a)). Sott's "failure to act" provides no action from which de facto suitability may be inferred. Nevertheless, Judge McLaughlin cites three cases as analogous to my case by which she seeks to "construct" de facto suitability from Sott's "failure to act." The cases are not analogous.

<u>Three cases cited as de facto determinations of suitability</u>
Attempting to "prove" de facto suitability, Judge McLaughlin, acting as "adjunct counsel for the defense," cites three cases, <u>Prehoda</u>,
<u>Edwards</u>, and <u>Botello</u> which, she claims, illustrate de facto suitabil-
ity analogous to my case (06-5325, p. 7). The analogies fail. The
three cases illustrate "agency action"--facts discernible to the sens-
es--from which de facto suitability may be <u>inferred</u>. In response to
my application, with its stated conviction, there is no IRS "agency
action." Instead of action, there is silence, the nonaction of Sott's
unlawful "failure to act" (5 U.S.C. 302(b)(8) (A) (i)), subject to
Court, not MSPB, review (5 U.S.C. 702).

# CHAPTER 18

# THE THREE CASES: PREHODA, EDWARDS, BOTELLO

1. <u>Prehoda v. Dep't of Homeland Security</u>, [DHS] 98 M.S.P.R. 418, 420-231 (M.S.P.B. 2005, hereinafter <u>Prehoda</u>)
2. <u>Edwards v. Dep't of Justice</u>, 87 M.S.P.R. 518, 522 (M.S.P.B. 2001, hereinafter <u>Edwards</u>)
3. <u>Botello v. Dep't of Justice</u>, 76 M.S.P.R. 117, 122 (M.S.P.B. 1997, hereinafter <u>Botello</u>)

## <u>PREHODA</u>

The right of appeal to the MSPB applies differently to complainants who are federal employees and to those who are not. Mr. Prehoda is a federal employee. I am not. Judge McLaughlin's analogy of <u>Prehoda</u> with my claim is therefore invalid. The MSPB has jurisdiction over appeals from federal employees because they are within the MSPB, administrative appeals process (5 C.F.R. 1201.3). Because I am not a federal employee, my "appeal" is not within MSPB process, with two exceptions: (1) my having been determined unsuitable (5 C.F.R. 1201.3 (a)(7)), and (2) my claiming discrimination in hiring (5 C.F.R. 1201.3(a)(19)).

I was not determined unsuitable, and I do not claim discrimination in hiring. Consequently, the exceptions are inapplicable. Sott, ignoring 5 C.F.R. 731.101, "erased" the requirement for suitability. In so doing she "erased" the jurisdiction of the MSPB and the right of MSPB appeal (5 C.F.R. 731.501(a)).

### Mr. Prehoda a federal employee

Mr. Prehoda, as a federal employee of the Immigration and Naturalization Service (INS), is therefore under MSPB jurisdiction. MSPB jurisdiction also arises from Mr. Prehoda's claim that his resignation from the INS was involuntary. "Involuntary resignation" is considered a "constructive removal," i.e., an "agency action," a fact perceivable to the senses, therefore grounds for MSPB appeal (Hammond v. Department of the Navy, 50 M.S.P.R. 174, affirmed, 954 F.2d 734 (Fed. Cir. 1991); Ogden v. Department of Commerce, 61 M.S.P.R. 36-7(1994).

Mr. Prehoda appealed his involuntary resignation to the MSPB. "His appeal was denied in part because the administrative law judge determined that some of Mr. Prehoda's testimony under oath was not credible" (Fed. Cir. Civil Action 05-3233, hereinafter 05-3233). (05-3233, p. 1).

Mr. Prehoda then sought employment with the Department of Homeland Security (DHS). "He was tentatively selected . . ." however the DHS withdrew the offer, "citing the prior determination that Mr. Prehoda had offered testimony that was not credible during his involuntary resignation hearing." David Prehoda v. Department of Homeland Security (05-3233, p. 2).

The DHS's overt citing of "not credible" testimony meets the suitability criterion of "intentional false statement" (5 C.F.R. 731.202(b)(3)). The DHS's overt citing is a perceivable "agency action," therefore basis for "construction" of de facto determination of suitability, therefore under MSPB jurisdiction.

Here we have three overt agency actions by the DHS: (1) tentative offer of selection for employment, (2) withdrawal of the offer, and (3) statement of "not credible testimony" as reason for the nonselection. Moreover, because of the tentative selection (later withdrawn), Mr. Prehoda had the status of federal employee. Owing to the DHS's <u>overt</u> agency actions, and Mr. Prehoda as federal employee, he is within the administrative (MSPB) appeals process.

In my case, nothing is overt. Due to the Selecting Officer's silent "failure to act," nothing is stated, neither "conviction," <u>objection</u>, nor <u>reason</u> from which may be inferred the existence of de facto suitability. In my case, only IRS silence and my immediate, unlawful removal from the selection process--absent determination of suitability, a violation of 5 U.S.C. 702 and 5 C.F.R. 731.101.

<u>"Not credible testimony" must equate with "conviction"</u>
For de facto suitability in <u>Prehoda</u> to be analogous to my case, Judge McLaughlin must demonstrate analogy of the DHS's <u>overt</u> statement of "not credible testimony" with Sott's <u>overt</u> statement of "conviction." Because Sott fraudulently concealed the stated conviction, no <u>overt</u> statement from Sott now acknowledging conviction is forthcoming. There is no demonstration of analogy.

Rather, Sott, with her "failure to act" and concealed conviction demonstrates de facto, deceptive nonhiring covered up with the lie of the "rule of three" as reason for nonhiring. Because there is no analogy between the DHS's <u>overt</u> statement of "not credible testimony" and Sott's <u>covert</u> concealment of "conviction," the "construction" of de facto determination of suitability is not possible. Nothing in <u>Prehoda</u> equates with Sott's "failure to act." Judge McLaughlin's <u>Prehoda</u> is a failed analogy.

## EDWARDS

Judge McLaughlin's second attempt at "proving" de facto suitability is the <u>Edwards</u> case (87 M.S.P.R. 518). Again, in <u>Edwards</u> there is <u>overt</u> "agency action" that supports construction of de facto determination. In my case the Selecting Officer's "failure to act" is absence of "agency action," which precludes construction of de facto determination.

Mr. Edwards, a preference eligible, applied for the position of Correctional Officer at the Federal Detention Center (FDC), Miami, Florida. He received the excellent rating of 99.0. The Selecting Officer then processed Standard Form (SF) 62, titled "Agency Request to Pass Over a Preference Eligible or Object to an Eligible," based on Mr. Edwards's supposed "qualifications" (87 M.S.P.R. 518, p. 2.).

### Overt agency action

The processing of SF 62 is an overt agency action to "pass over" (not select) Mr. Edwards. The FDC then requested that Mr. Edwards's "name be removed from the certificate of eligibles based on his "qualifications." The request is yet another overt agency action, a fact stated in writing.

According to the FDC, the term "qualifications" refers to Mr. Edwards's apparent failure to reveal a termination from a previous federal job. The FDC claimed Mr. Edwards failed to follow office procedures and dress code, and lack of "dependability, stability, maturity, responsibility, and reliability necessary to perform Correctional Officer duties" (87 M.S.P.R. 518, p. 2.). The "qualifications" were thus stated, another overt agency action, a discernible fact.

Mr. Edwards appealed to the MSPB claiming that his pass-over, allegedly based on qualifications, was actually based on factors pertaining to suitability. If indeed suitability, the FDC's overt accusations provide ground for the construction of de facto suitability. In my case, Sott's "failure to act," is lack of overt agency action, thus no possible construction of de facto suitability. Absent IRS action, Judge McLaughlin's analogy of Edwards with my case fails.

The MSPB dismissed Mr. Edwards's appeal for lack of jurisdiction stating, "the agency's express reason for its action was a concern about the appellant's qualifications, not his suitability." Considering Mr. Edwards's rating of 99.0, it is unlikely that "qualifications" is reason for the pass-over.

Mr. Edwards then appealed the MSPB's dismissal to the Central Board which held that the agency's <u>reasons</u> for the pass-over apply to the "character or conduct of a candidate." The <u>reasons</u> "were of the sort normally relied upon in making suitability determinations" (87 M.S.P.R. 518, p. 5). The Central Board remanded Mr. Edwards's appeal to the MSPB for a jurisdictional hearing.

The FDC's processing of SF 62 is an <u>overt</u> agency action. In my case, Sott did <u>not</u> object, provided <u>no</u> reason to the OPM, and processed <u>no</u> forms. The <u>Edwards</u> case provides overt agency action which supports the "construction" of de facto determination of suitability. In my case there is no agency action, only inaction--Sott's "failure to act."

Nonexistent agency action precludes both de facto suitability and right of appeal to the MSPB (5 C.F.R. 1201.3(a)(1-21)). Instead, "failure to act" is subject to <u>Court</u> review (5 U.S.C. 702). Judge McLaughlin's attempt to analogize the FDC's <u>overt</u> SF 62 pass-over with the IRS's <u>covert</u> "failure to act" is without substance. One wonders if she read the <u>Edwards</u> case. Her attempted analogy of <u>Edwards</u> with my case fails.

## BOTELLO

Judge McLaughlin, arguing <u>Botello</u> as de facto suitability analogous to my case, could not possibly have read the <u>Botello</u> case (76 M.S.P.R. 117). In addition to defending Sott's "failure to act," she ignores the essential difference between <u>Botello</u> and my case. That is, Mr. Botello claims the MSPB <u>has</u> jurisdiction, while I claim the MSPB <u>lacks</u> the jurisdiction held by her Court (28 U.S.C. 1331). Her citing <u>Botello</u> as analogy is a leap into fantasy. Moreover, the MSPB has jurisdiction over <u>Botello</u> because of Mr. Botello's status of former veteran.

Being a former veteran (also claiming discrimination), Mr. Botello is given the right of appeal within the administrative (MSPB) process pursuant to the Uniformed Services Employment and Reemployment Rights Act USERRA). (76 M.S.P.R. 117, p.2).

Mr. Botello alleged that the United States Marshals Service "cancelled his selection . . . based on suitability." He appealed to the MSPB which dismissed the appeal for lack of jurisdiction, stating, "appellant's claim was in the nature of a nonselection, over which the Board has no jurisdiction" (76 M.S.P.R. 117, p. 3). The dismissal was remanded for discovery (Central Board, 76 M.S.P.R. 117, p. 6).

### Mr. Botello was informed by the agency of his unsuitability

Mr. Botello alleged that his selection for employment was cancelled because of "unfavorable information" uncovered in a preliminary background check, and was so informed by the agency (76 M.S.P.R 117, p. 4). Informing Mr. Botello of "unfavorable information" is an "agency action," a perceivable fact, therefore ground for "construction" of de facto determination of suitability.

Furthermore, the agency mentioned the term "unsuitability," another overt "agency action." Merely mentioning "unsuitability," supports Mr. Botello's claim ". . . that the agency made a suitability determination" (76 M.S.P.R. 117, p 4). Informing Mr. Botello of "unfavorable information," and mentioning "unsuitability," are factual, overt agency actions which support "construction" of de facto determination of suitability.

In my case, the IRS never informed me that I was denied a position because of "unfavorable information." In response to my requests for the reason for nonhiring, IRS employees state the "rule of three" as reason, their standard lie, knowing "three considerations" were never implemented.

Contrary to Judge McLaughlin's claim of de facto determination of suitability, Sott's "failure to act" precludes any action or statement that might be construed as de facto determination, with MSPB jurisdiction. Failing to act and omitting suitability, Sott fraudulently nullified MSPB jurisdiction and right of MSPB appeal. Botello shares nothing with my case. Botello is a failed analogy.

## Three cases, three failed analogies

Judge McLaughlin's three cases of overt agency action provide no analogy with IRS's covert "failure to act" which omits agency action. Based on the Able Assistant's "research," Judge McLaughlin attempted to prove de facto suitability therefore MSPB jurisdiction. Despite the "research," she did not--because she could not--demonstrate analogy of the three cases' overt agency actions with Sott's covert "failure to act," which precludes overt agency action. Therefore no de facto unsuitability. Consequently no MSPB jurisdiction. Judge McLaughlin's failure to demonstrate analogy discredits her claim of de facto suitability. Rather, she demonstrates her unethical role of "adjunct counsel for the defense," defending the IRS's violations of law in order to evade review of a lawful cause of action.

How is it, with the massive number of complaints concerning agency employment practices, Judge McLaughlin did not cite a single law or precedent of MSPB jurisdiction over the nonhiring of an applicant who is not presently a federal employee, and who is not determined unsuitable? No doubt because no such law or precedent exists.

## Charade of administrative remedies, "absurd" Fed. Cir. appeal

Judge McLaughlin's dismissal of the refiling (06-5325) protects the IRS from judicial review. Absent determination of suitability, the MSPB lacks jurisdiction (5 C.F.R. 1201.3(a)(7)). The MSPB's dismissal is therefore lawful. Appealing a lawful dismissal to the Fed. Cir. is absurd. The "appeal" a charade, the result of the doctrine of "exhaustion of administrative remedies" applied to my nonadministrative complaint. The Fed. Cir. will <u>not</u> reverse MSPB's dismissal. The doctrine applied to a nonadministrative complaint is a sterile process that delays the judicial process provided under the APA, namely, Court review of the IRS's "failure to act" (5 U.S.C. 702) and IRS's unlawful nullification of required suitability (5 C.F.R. 731.101).

# CHAPTER 19

# ABSURD "APPEAL" TO THE FED. CIR.

Unappealable "appeal" to the Fed. Cir.

"Failure to select . . . is generally not appealable to the Board" (Prewitt v. MSPB), therefore not appealable to the Fed. Cir. Yet, being required to appeal the MSPB'S lawful dismissal, on date October 11, 2007, I appealed a lawful MSPB dismissal, an absurd exercise, to the Fed. Cir. I submitted the Notice of Appeal of the MSPB's lawful dismissal (PH-0731) to the Fed. Cir. Pursuant to procedure, I submitted the Notice on Fed. Cir. Form 1, by way of the Clerk of Court, Eastern District of Pennsylvania. The appeal, empty, a matter of form.

Notice of Appeal misdirected by the Clerk of Court

The Notice was mishandled by the Clerk of Court. Instead of transmitting the Notice to the Fed. Cir., she docketed the Notice at the Third Cir., the court that lacks subject matter jurisdiction over MSPB appeals. I advised the clerk to submit the Notice to the Fed. Cir. She would do so and would so notify me. She submitted the Notice to the Fed. Cir. but failed to notify. The Notice was now at both the Third Cir. and the Fed. Cir., with the Third Cir. having a thirty-day lead time in the process. At that point, I failed to grasp the significance of the difference between subject matter and personal jurisdiction.

Because the Third Cir., had a thirty-day lead time, and personal jurisdiction over me, I thought it expedient that the "appeal" remain at the Third Cir. Therefore, I withdrew the "appeal" from the Fed. Cir., erroneously, because the Third Cir. lacked the required subject matter jurisdiction. The Third Cir. "ruled" that Judge McLaughlin's Court lacks the subject matter jurisdiction held by the Fed. Cir. (07-4042, August 15, 2008, p. 3, hereinafter 07-4042). No matter the ruling, Third Cir., lacking subject matter jurisdiction, its "ruling," is <u>void</u> at its making.

<u>Judge McLaughlin falsely claims Third Cir. jurisdiction</u>
During the period of "appeals"--July 30, 2005, MSPB (PH-0731) to August 15, 2008 Third Cir. (07-4042)--both MSPB and Third Cir. lack subject matter jurisdiction. Lacking jurisdiction, they lack the power to render a valid, final judgment on the issues. Judge McLaughlin's claim of "valid and final judgment" by the Third Cir. (09-5941, p. 8)--while she simultaneously claims Fed. Cir. "exclusive jurisdiction" (06-5325, p. 6)--is false on its face. The period July 30, 2005-August 15, 2008 was a waste of time and effort both for me and, regretfully, the Third Cir., which endured the erroneous "appeal."

<u>Time period for submission of appeal to the Fed. Cir. elapsed</u>
Meanwhile, the sixty-day period for appeal to the Fed. Cir. elapsed. The contradictory "exhaustion" of <u>nonexistent</u> "administrative remedies" yet to be completed.

# CHAPTER 20

# RESTART APPEAL PROCESS

### Appeal to the Fed. Cir. follows appeal to the MSPB

In order to reestablish the sixty-day time period for "appealing" the absurdity of a <u>lawful</u> MSPB dismissal to the Fed. Cir., on date January 29, 2009, I submitted to the MSPB the identical, so-called "appeal" formerly submitted July 30, 2005 (PH-0731). The former "appeal" was dismissed November 28, 2005 for lack of subject matter jurisdiction. Lack of jurisdiction nullifies power of rendering valid, final decision. Thus, under PH-0731, the MSPB decided no issues.

### Collateral estoppel

The second "appeal," as was the first, is dismissible for lack of jurisdiction. Yet, a different ALJ, Lystra A. Harris, dismissed on ground of "collateral estoppel" under PH-0752-09-0251-I-1, March 27, 2009 (hereinafter PH-0752), false ground. Collateral estoppel <u>bars</u> relitigating a <u>decided</u> issue. Dismissal for lack of jurisdiction under PH-0731 means <u>no</u> issues were decided, therefore no bar. She may only dismiss for lack of jurisdiction as under PH-0731.

Apparently, ALJ Harris understands jurisdiction <u>itself</u> as the "issue" of a complaint against the MSPB, with the MSPB somehow replacing the IRS as respondent. Only with such faulty understanding does she claim collateral estoppel. She creates a "fantasy-jurisdiction-as-issue" and substitutes it for the issue of deceptive IRS nonhiring--a muddle. Moreover, no matter how she understands process, jurisdiction itself is <u>not</u> subject to principles of estoppel.

Collateral estoppel bars relitigation of the <u>issues</u> validly decided in a previous litigation in a court of competent jurisdiction. The MSPB is not a court and has no jurisdiction. The ALJ under PH-0731 did not decide issues of IRS violations. Instead he <u>lawfully</u> dismissed for lack of jurisdiction. Thus, ALJ Harris's dismissal (PH-0752) on ground of collateral estoppel is meaningless. Nevertheless, her dismissal, per se, is "correct" because, absent determination of <u>unsuitability</u>, the MSPB has no jurisdiction over my complaint (5 C.F.R. 731.501(a)) and has no part in it.

### Collateral estoppel irrelevant to MSPB lack of jurisdiction

ALJ Harris's dismissal "confirms" the MSPB's prior dismissal (PH-0731) for lack of jurisdiction. MSPB jurisdiction lacks in PH-0752, as in PH-0731 the "appeals" being identical. The sole purpose of the latter "appeal" (PH-0752) was to restart the clock for timely "appeal" to the Fed. Cir., which it did.

# CHAPTER 21

# FED. CIR. AND MSPB JURISDICTION

<u>Fed. Cir. validates the MSPB's lack of jurisdiction</u>

On date May 2, 2009 I submitted to the Fed. Cir. the "appeal" dismissed by ALJ Harris on false grounds of collateral estoppel (PH-0752). Fed. Cir. affirmed ALJ Harris's dismissal and, significantly, did <u>not</u> reverse the MSPB's former dismissal under PH-0731 for lack of jurisdiction (Fed. Cir. Civil Action 2009-3187, October 9, 2009, hereinafter, 2009-3187). Lack of jurisdiction under PH-0731 remains, which falsifies ALJ Harris's claim of "collateral estoppel" (PH-0752).

The Fed. Cir.'s accepting the MSPB's lack of jurisdiction means "administrative remedies" do <u>not</u> exist. Therefore, the wild-goose chase of exhausting nonexistent administrative remedies (5 C.F.R. 731.501(a)), part of the IRS's deceptive, unlawful personnel practice, is ended.

# CHAPTER 22

# THE COURT'S TEMPORARY LACK OF JURISDICTION

### Court "lacks" jurisdiction during administrative (MSPB) process

Claiming lack of jurisdiction prior to Fed. Cir. decision, MSPB, Court and Third Cir. claim lack of power to render a final decision on the issues of IRS deceptive nonhiring practice. Judge McLaughlin's later claim of valid "final decision" by MSPB and Third Cir.--both lacking jurisdiction--is blatantly false. Her claim of issue preclusion is therefore also false. The issues of the IRS's deceptive, unlawful nonhiring practice remain undecided.

### Jurisdiction of the Court (28 U.S.C. 1331) effectuated

The Fed. Cir.'s accepting MSPB's lack of jurisdiction proves the complaint is outside the administrative (MSPB) appeals process. There are no "administrative remedies" to "exhaust." Sott's "failure to act" unlawfully conceals "conviction," thus "erases" both suitability and 5 C.F.R. 731.501(a) which protects the IRS from MSPB appeal in the event of determination of unsuitability.

The administrative (MSPB) process is inapplicable to Sott's "failure to act," a legal wrong for which the APA provides judicial--not MSPB--review (5 U.S.C. 702). Absent determination of negative suitability, the MSPB lacks jurisdiction (5 C.F.R. 731.501(a)). It is the Court in which Judge McLaughlin presides that has original jurisdiction (28 U.S.C. 1331), the jurisdiction she brazenly denies.

# CHAPTER 23

# REENTERED COMPLAINT AT COURT

<u>Absent administrative remedies, complaint refiled at Court</u>
Absent administrative remedies, and pursuant to Judge Giles's dismissal <u>without</u> <u>prejudice</u> (04-4876), on date November 30, 2009 I refiled the complaint of IRS deceptive, unlawful nonhiring practice at federal district court (09-5941, <u>Muhammad v. Carlson</u>; <u>Barnes v. Chatterton</u>).

<u>Judge McLaughlin's switcheroo dismissal (09-5941)</u>
Judge McLaughlin, on April 26, 2010, dismissed, claiming ground of issue preclusion--but in fact dismissed on ground of lack of jurisdiction--a fraudulent change of ground, therefore a fraudulent dismissal by a district court judge! Issue preclusion and lack of jurisdiction are mutually exclusive. They do not coexist.

"Issue preclusion" is the <u>barring</u> of the relitigation of issues of a complaint that were brought to a final decision in a court of competent jurisdiction. (American Law Institute, Restatement, Judgments, Section 45). All of Judge McLaughlin's dismissals were for lack of jurisdiction (06-5325), meaning she made no final decision on the issues. Therefore, issue preclusion is not applicable. Her phony "issue preclusion/lack of jurisdiction" dismissal (09-5941) is a sham.

Judge McLaughlin is well aware of the contradiction of <u>barring</u> for issue preclusion but dismissing for lack of jurisdiction. Claiming lack of jurisdiction, she never made a final decision, therefore she could not lawfully bar. Instead, she dismissed for lack of jurisdiction (09-5941, pp. 8, 9), a switch of ground, a fraud, the brazen ploy of a judge of the federal district court who buries her deceitful cases unpublished. Public protection from judicial fraud requires public awareness. Exposing Judge McLaughlin's fraudulent adjudication is a public service.

## Simultaneous existence of "issue preclusion" and "lack of jurisdiction"?

Judge McLaughlin, referring to MSPB "appeal" PH-0752 (09-5941, p. 4), makes the outrageous argument that the "issues" of the complaint "had already been fully litigated in his previous MSPB [PH-0731] proceeding." Here she fuses MSPB with Court, and uses the term "fully litigated" as substitute for "final decision" to confuse, to deceive, to argue my complaint is decided by MSPB "final decision" as though MSPB is the Court. <u>All</u> prior dismissals--except Judge Giles's "without prejudice" (04-4876)--were for lack of jurisdiction; this means <u>no</u> valid final decision either by MSPB or Court on issues of IRS unlawful nonhiring.

The MSPB is not a court of law, has no jurisdiction over my "appeal" (5 C.F.R. 1201.3(a)(7), and dismisses for <u>lack</u> of jurisdiction (PH-0731) accepted by the Fed. Cir. Judge McLaughlin's "fully litigated" argument is an attempt to deceive. Evading review, she dismisses on false claim of lack of jurisdiction, ignoring 28 U.S.C. 1331. Evading jurisdiction and review, she "fully litigated" nothing.

## Scam dismissal, a mockery of judicial procedure

Piggy-backing on ALJ Harris's muddled dismissal based on a non-existent "collateral estoppel" (PH-0752), Judge McLaughlin, claiming issue preclusion, mixes administrative and judicial roles to obscure her evasion of review.

Because she dismissed for lack of jurisdiction (06-5325), she knows her claim of issue preclusion (09-5941) is false. Therefore, instead of <u>barring</u> for issue preclusion she dismissed for lack of jurisdiction (09-5941), a scam. Judge McLaughlin's handling of this case makes a mockery of lawful, judicial procedure. Her claim of "issue preclusion" stating PH-0752 and 06-5325 is a fraud.

Dismissing for lack of jurisdiction (09-5941) <u>after</u> Fed. Cir. let stand MSPB's lack of jurisdiction, she dismisses unlawfully, violating 28 U.S.C. 1331. Her Court is venue for review of wrongful agency action pursuant to statute and precedent: 5 U.S.C. 702, 704; 28 U.S.C. 1331; 430 U.S. 99, 105, 1977; 487 U.S. 879, 891 n 16, 1988; 520 U.S. 154, 175 (1997); 345 F. 3d 216 (Third Cir. 2003)).

<u>Three conditions required for claiming "issue preclusion" under 09-5941</u>
Judge McLaughlin's claim of "Issue preclusion" requires the following:

1. The issues must first be litigated to a valid final decision, not dismissed for lack of jurisdiction (06-5325)
2. The issues, having been validly decided, arc attcmpted to be relitigated in a subsequent, <u>different</u> litigation
3. The issues, having been validly decided, are then <u>barred </u>from relitigation

<u>Absent final decision, litigation continues, no relitigation</u>
Judge McLaughlin dismissing for lack of jurisdiction (06-5325), made no valid, final decision. Absent valid, final decision, there is no different, subsequent relitigation to be barred under 09-5941. Absent barring, refiling resumes litigation of undecided issues (<u>Muhammad v. Carlson</u>; <u>Barnes v. Chatterton)</u>. Continually dismissing for lack of jurisdiction, she cannot credibly claim issue preclusion.

# CHAPTER 24

# THE HOAX: FINAL DECISION, "ACTUALLY LITIGATED AND RESOLVED"

### Judge McLaughlin doubles down on the hoax of "final decision"

At 09-5941, p. 5, Judge McLaughlin states the complaint "was actually litigated and resolved in an earlier litigation" i.e., 06-5325. Under 06-5325 she dismissed for lack of jurisdiction, as she later dismissed for lack of jurisdiction under 09-5941. Claiming lack of jurisdiction in both, she resolved nothing. She substitutes the term "actually litigated and resolved" for "valid, final decision," an unconscionable attempt to deceive.

### "Actually litigated and resolved"?

"Actually litigated" is what takes place in a court. Litigation may lead to valid, final decision and resolution, or to dismissal for lack of jurisdiction absent decision and resolution. "Resolved" pertains to the Court's final decision on issues of IRS violations, e.g., "failure to act," "fraudulent concealment of "conviction," omission of "suitability, et al. Such decision resolves the issues and ends the litigation. Because Judge McLaughlin dismissed for lack of jurisdiction (06-5325), she did <u>not</u> decide the issues. Her claim to "resolved" issues of IRS violations is false, as well she knows. The issues remain unresolved.

### No final decision means no bar to refiling
Had there been a valid "final decision," and had there been a subsequent claim with the "issues" previously decided, Judge McLaughlin would have <u>barred</u> the refiling on ground of issue preclusion. However, she did <u>not</u> bar because she knows she made <u>no</u> "final decision." Unable to lawfully bar, she dismissed on ground of lack of jurisdiction, a fraudulent, unconscionable change of grounds. Dismissing for lack of jurisdiction (09-5941) belies her claim of issue preclusion.

### Complaint not subject to the administrative (MSPB) appeals process
Absent applicant unsuitability, MSPB lacks jurisdiction over the IRS's nonhiring an applicant who is not a federal employee (5 C.F.R. 1201.3(a)(7)). I am not a federal employee. Owing to the IRS's unlawful omission of suitability, my complaint is not within the administrative (MSPB) appeals process. It is within the judicial process (28 U.S.C. 1331), unlawfully evaded by Judge McLaughlin.

# CHAPTER 25

# NO CASE FOR ISSUE PRECLUSION

## A strategy for avoiding review

The Fed. Cir.'s acceptance of MSPB's dismissal for lack of jurisdiction (2009-3187) ends the charade of exhausting nonexistent administrative remedies. Prior to Fed. Cir. ruling, Judge McLaughlin, dismissing for lack of jurisdiction, made no final decision on the issues of the IRS's unlawful nonhiring practice. Absent final decision, the refiling November 30, 2009 (09-5941) does not relitigate the complaint. It continues the unresolved complaint in its lawful venue--her Court.

Claiming "issue preclusion," Judge McLaughlin must show the attempt to relitigate a valid final decision in a subsequent, different claim. Dismissing for lack of jurisdiction, she made no valid, final decision on IRS violations. Thus no subsequent, different claim. Absent final decision, the issues remain unresolved. Because she cannot lawfully claim issue preclusion, she dismisses on ground of lack of jurisdiction (09-5941, April 26, 2010)--a tacit admission her claim of issue preclusion is a fraud.

## Judge McLaughlin "creates" retroactive Third Cir. jurisdiction

Judge McLaughlin, defending her lack-of-jurisdiction dismissal, craftily creates Third Cir. retroactive jurisdiction to claim as valid the Third Cir.'s earlier <u>void</u>, invalid "ruling" of Court lack of jurisdiction. She "confers" jurisdiction upon the Third Cir.--simultaneously claiming Fed. Cir. has <u>exclusive</u> jurisdiction! She gets deeper and deeper into the muck of her tortuous, denial of her Court's jurisdiction.

The Third Cir., which lacks the jurisdiction held by the Fed. Cir., is present in this case solely a result of the Clerk of Court's erroneous docketing my appeal at the Third Cir. The Third Cir. responded (07-4042), stating the Fed. Cir. has jurisdiction, thus confirming its own lack of jurisdiction (09-5941. P. 8). Lack of jurisdiction means the Third Cir. has no lawful power to render a "valid, final decision." Therefore, decision by the Third Cir. is void at its making. It is the Fed. Cir. that has jurisdiction over appeals of MSPB decisions (5 U.S.C. 7703). The Third Cir., lacking jurisdiction, is out of the picture.

Nevertheless, Judge McLaughlin will attempt to prove "issue preclusion," not on the issues of IRS violations she never decided, but on the Third Cir.'s <u>void</u> "ruling" that Fed. Cir., not her Court, has jurisdiction (09-5941, p. 7). The void "ruling" is dated August 15, 2008 (07-4042), <u>prior</u> to Fed. Cir. ruling October 9, 2009 (2009-3187). In the cases, <u>Yeboah v. DOJ</u> and <u>Fairview Township v. EPA</u> in which Third Cir. <u>has</u> jurisdiction, it ruled her Court has the jurisdiction she denies. She argues the impossible. Her creation of retroactive Third Cir. jurisdiction is a judicial scam. Without doubt, her Court has <u>original</u> jurisdiction (28 U.S.C. 1331). Claiming Third Cir. jurisdiction--while the Third Cir. itself states the Fed. Cir. has exclusive jurisdiction--Judge McLaughlin, from the outset, beginning with Sott's "failure to act," evinces her obsession of evading her lawful duty of review (5 U.S.C. 702). She cannot prove issue preclusion while dismissing for lack of jurisdiction, an attempt to defraud.

<u>Fed. Cir. valid and final judgment?</u>

Judge McLaughlin argues that Third Cir. "ruling" on Fed. Cir. jurisdiction is "a valid and final judgment [06-5325] that determined the issue of this Court's jurisdiction" (09-5941, p.8). She misleads. The <u>issue</u> is IRS violations. Lacking jurisdiction, Third Cir. "ruling" is <u>void</u>, determines nothing. Fed. Cir. accepts MSPB <u>lack</u> of jurisdiction, which "affirms" Court jurisdiction. Claiming "issue preclusion" on Third Cir. <u>void</u> ruling she sullies her judgeship. If jurisdiction is a settled IRS "issue," she should <u>bar</u> jurisdiction, which is nonsensical, revealing the deceit of her argument. Issue preclusion is nonexistent. Therefore she did not bar, but dismissed for lack of jurisdiction, a violation of 28 U.S.C. 1331.

Although Third Cir. is in this case by Clerk of Court error, it brings with it the fresh air of clarity by stating the Fed. Cir. has jurisdiction to decide an <u>appeal</u> of MSPB decision. Fed. Cir. decision ends the impossible quest of exhausting nonexistent, administrative remedies. Judge McLaughlin deceives, claiming Third Cir. jurisdiction--while she simultaneously claims the Fed. Cir. has <u>exclusive</u> jurisdiction (06-5325, p. 5)! Dismissing for lack of jurisdiction, she <u>knows</u> she did not render a valid final decision on the issue of IRS deceptive, unlawful nonhiring practice. IRS violations, e.g., failure to act, concealment of conviction, unlawful omission of suitability remain undecided while she argues deceptively as "adjunct counsel for the defense," shielding the IRS, in order to evade her duty of review.

### <u>Third Cir. comment on appellate, not district court jurisdiction</u>

Third Cir. lacks jurisdiction because the complaint was forced into the MSPB process pursuant to Judge Giles's applying the doctrine of the "exhaustion of administrative remedies." Nevertheless, it is noted that the Third Cir.'s void comment regards <u>appellate</u> jurisdiction of the Fed. Cir., not the <u>original</u> jurisdiction assigned Judge McLaughlin's Court by law (28 U.S.C. 1331), which she unlawfully ignores. No wonder she did not publish the case.

## Administrative remedies exhausted, Court has jurisdiction

Judge McLaughlin's argument of Court lacking jurisdiction is discredited when the Fed. Cir. let stand the MSPB's claim of lack of MSPB jurisdiction (2009-3187). At that instant, "administrative remedies" are shown to be nonexistent. Thus, the refiling at Court (09-5941) is lawful. Prior to Fed. Cir. decision, Judge McLaughlin may claim lack of Court jurisdiction, but not subsequent Fed. Cir. decision. Pursuant to statute (28 U.S.C. 1331) and precedent (Califano v. Sanders; Bowen v. Massachussetts; Yeboah v. DOJ; Fairview Township v. EPA), her Court has the jurisdiction she brazenly denies.

## Displacement of the issue of IRS violations with "jurisdiction-as-issue"

Judge McLaughlin displaces the issue of IRS unlawful nonhiring practice with a fabricated "jurisdiction-as-issue" as the issue of my complaint against the IRS. She then claims her fabrication is subject to issue preclusion. Actually, she reflects the ALJ's muddled claim of "jurisdiction" as being the issue against the MSPB subject to "collateral estoppel" (PH-0752). Judge McLaughlin takes the ALJ's muddle and runs with it, using it for her phony "issue preclusion" argument--phony because she did not bar for issue preclusion but dismissed for lack of jurisdiction, a blatant scam. This is one devious, unscrupulous judge.

The IRS's violation of lawful employment procedure is the issue subject to judicial--not MSPB--review (28 U.S.C. 1331). Judge McLaughlin defends IRS violations by substituting in their place a false "jurisdiction-as-issue," and false "issue preclusion," deceptions to cover her unlawful evasion of review.

## "Jurisdiction-as-issue," a cover-up of IRS violation-as-issue

Judge McLaughlin displaces the issue of IRS unlawful nonhiring with the ALJ's fabricated "jurisdiction-as-issue" (PH-0752), then applies "issue preclusion" to the fabrication. She claims issue preclusion as ground for dismissal, but dismisses for lack of jurisdiction, a judicial fraud. Issue preclusion is antithetical to dismissal for lack of jurisdiction. Issue preclusion is ground for <u>barring</u> a complaint from relitigation (09-5941). The question is "why did she not bar?"

### No "issue preclusion," therefore my claim not barred

Issue preclusion is applicable when issues are brought to a final decision in a court of competent jurisdiction and a party later attempts to relitigate the issues under a different claim. The issues having been decided, the second attempt is <u>barred</u> from relitigation. Judge McLaughlin, continually dismissing for lack of jurisdiction, never settled the issues. Therefore, she could not lawfully bar, and indeed did not. Instead, she dismissed for lack of jurisdiction--unlawfully, by fiat--while claiming issue preclusion as ground, an outright, fraudulent dismissal.

Judge McLaughlin resorts to outlandish fantasies to prove issue preclusion, even the fantasy of creating retroactive jurisdiction of the Third Cir. so as to validate it's void ruling of lack of Court jurisdiction. All this while the Third Cir. itself states Fed. Cir.--not Third Cir.--has jurisdiction.

### Judge McLaughlin's modus operandi: deception

Judge McLaughlin claims the MSPB (PH-0752) which lacks jurisdiction, has jurisdiction over jurisdiction itself, a deception masking the jurisdiction assigned her Court by Article III, Section 2 of the Constitution, and by statute (28 U.S.C. 1331). She "creates" retroactive Third Cir. jurisdiction, while claiming Fed. Cir. has "exclusive jurisdiction." She refers to ALJ Harris's muddled claim of collateral estoppel under PH-0752 as valid--a farce in face of the MSPB's prior dismissal for lack of jurisdiction (PH-0731). She claims issue preclusion but dismisses for lack of jurisdiction--plain fraud. This is a judge evading jurisdiction, defending the IRS by deception because IRS violations cannot be defended by claiming them lawful.

### Judge McLaughlin hides her unlawful evasion of review

This case must be one of the top award-winning travesties of adjudication by a judge of U.S. District Court, Eastern District, Pennsylvania. Judge McLaughlin knows her arguments are phony, embarrassing if brought to light. Thus, she labels the case "non-precedential," does not publish it, avoiding public embarrassment.

# CHAPTER 26

# AUTHORITY FOR CLAIMING ISSUE PRECLUSION

Judge McLaughlin cites authority for claiming issue preclusion

Claiming "issue preclusion," Judge McLaughlin cites as authority a case filed in the United States District Court for the Western District of Pennsylvania: "Ins. Corp. of Ireland, Ltd. v. Compagnie des Bauxites de Guinea, 456 U.S. 694, 702 n. 9 (1982) (principles of preclusion apply to determinations of subject matter jurisdiction))." (Hereinafter Ins. Co. of Ireland v. Compagnie Des Bauxites.)

Judge McLaughlin "determines" subject matter jurisdiction?
Note Judge McLaughlin's parenthetical comment, "principles of preclusion apply to determinations of subject matter jurisdiction." Why the comment? No doubt because they do not apply to subject matter jurisdiction. Court has subject matter jurisdiction by statute (28 U.S.C. 1331) not by her "determinations." Preclusion applies to relitigation of issues of IRS violations validly decided in prior litigation. The issues were not decided, because Judge McLaughlin, dismissing for lack of jurisdiction, never rendered a valid, final decision, thus no issue preclusion.

## Ins. Co. of Ireland v. Compagnie Des Bauxites--personal jurisdiction

Fact: Ins. Co. of Ireland v. Compagnie Des Bauxites concerns personal jurisdiction, not the subject matter jurisdiction which pertains to my case. Ins. Co. of Ireland, responding to a claim against it, raised a defense of lack of personal jurisdiction. Compagnie Des Bauxites attempted to use discovery to establish jurisdictional facts. Because Compagnie Des Bauxites failed to produce the requested information, the district court, pursuant to Civil Procedure Rule 37(b)(2)(A), asserted personal jurisdiction over defendant for a fair hearing. In contrast, subject matter jurisdiction is not subject to "assertion." It is assigned to the Court by Constitution (Article III, Section II) and statute (28 U.S.C. 1331).

## Personal jurisdiction asserted, subject matter jurisdiction unlawfully negated

The judge in Ins. Co. of Ireland v. Compagnie Des Bauxites lawfully asserted personal jurisdiction. In my case, Judge McLaughlin unlawfully negated the subject matter jurisdiction assigned her Court by Constitution, statute, and precedent. Subject matter jurisdiction, not personal jurisdiction, applies to my case.

## Judge McLaughlin cannot lawfully bar my claim against the IRS

Issue preclusion may not be applied absent final decision on the issues, and absent a different, subsequent claim on the same issues. Never deciding the issues, Judge McLaughlin could not lawfully bar my claim for "issue preclusion." Consequently, she dismissed for lack of jurisdiction but claimed "issue preclusion" as ground a contradiction and a mockery of lawful dismissal (09-5941). Judge McLaughlin's citing Ins. Co. of Ireland v. Compagnie Des Bauxites--which concerns personal jurisdiction--reveals the falsity of her argument which concerns her Court's subject matter jurisdiction.

## Judge McLaughlin's fabricated "jurisdiction-as-issue/issue preclusion," a sham

Subject matter jurisdiction under 28 U.S.C. 1331 is not an "issue" to be barred in a later litigation. The issue to be barred, were it previously decided, is IRS violation of employment law, which Judge McLaughlin <u>never</u> decided. Instead, she uses ALJ Harris's muddle of "jurisdiction-as-issue/collateral/estoppel" as cover up of Court jurisdiction and absence of Court decision. Arguing un-ethically as "adjunct counsel for the defense," she obscures IRS violations with a fabricated "MSPB jurisdiction-as-issue," a ploy to confuse, to evade reviewing IRS "failure to act" (5 U.S.C. 702; 5 U.S.C. 2302 (b)(A)(i)) and unlawful circumvention of suitability (5 C.F.R. 731.101).

Judge McLaughlin dismissing for lack of jurisdiction omits fi-nal decision on issue of IRS violations, yet falsely claims issue pre-clusion on the undecided issue. Craftily she displaces the issue of IRS violation with the fabricated issue of "jurisdiction-as-issue, then dismisses the fabrication claiming issue preclusion but in fact dismisses for lack of jurisdiction, one obfuscating scam.

# CHAPTER 27

# SUMMARY

### IRS employees benefit from their unlawful personnel practice

Sott, motivated by "efficiency," and convenience of omitting suitability, immediately drops from consideration an applicant who stated derogatory information (conviction) in his application. She simply fails to act (5 U.S.C. 702) as though the application did not exist, a violation (5 U.S.C. 2302(b) (8)(A)(i)). "Efficiency" leads to salary increase. Profit from violating law, defended by Richard J. Cronin, Director, IRS Personnel Services. How good does it get?

### Judge McLaughlin's fraudulent adjudication, a rigged system

With Judge McLaughlin's fraudulent dismissal for lack of jurisdiction, I ceased further action. A district court judge who gets away with a fraudulent dismissal means a judicially rigged system. The case ends with a lying IRS protected by a deceiving district court judge intent on evading review by denying the jurisdiction of her Court (28 U.S.C. 1331). She defends Sott's "failure to act" and refuses review of a lawful cause of action, my complaint.

Judge McLaughlin incredibly attempts to create retroactive Third Cir. jurisdiction in order to create Third Cir. authorization for her claim of lack of jurisdiction. Claiming Third Cir. jurisdiction--while she simultaneously claims Fed. Cir. "exclusive jurisdiction"--is a sham. She uses the term "fully litigated" as meaning "valid final decision," a sham. She dismisses the complaint claiming issue preclusion as ground, but dismisses on ground of lack of jurisdiction, a sham. All her arguments in defense of the IRS are attempts to deceive, every argument a sham.

Because IRS violations, e.g., failure to act, omission of suitability are unlawful, they cannot be proved lawful. Judge McLaughlin attempts such proof and fails. She failed to prove MSPB jurisdiction. She failed to create de facto suitability. Complicit with the IRS, she accepted Sott's perjurious declarations. Her adjudication, replete with judicial fraud, she labeled "nonprecedential" and failed to publish it, hiding it. She trashes judicial ethics, negates her Court's jurisdiction, defends IRS violations, and, with a fraudulent dismissal, evades review.

### Judge McLaughlin's fantasies
Obsessed with evading review, Judge McLaughlin creates fantasies, namely, direct appeal, <u>invisible</u> de facto suitability, MSPB jurisdiction-as-issue displacing IRS violations of law as issue, principles of preclusion apply to subject matter jurisdiction when they do not, dismissal claimed on ground of issue preclusion but dismissing for lack of jurisdiction--all of it unconscionable fraud.

### Acting as "adjunct counsel for the defense," Judge McLaughlin "wins"
Judge McLaughlin "wins" this case, not lawfully but by fiat dismissal on false ground. She claims dismissal on false ground of issue preclusion, but in fact dismisses on false ground of lack of jurisdiction--two false "grounds." Violating Constitution, statute, and precedent she denies her Court's jurisdiction thereby unlawfully evades review. Arguing as "adjunct counsel for the defense,"

she aids the IRS in cheating applicant of the right to the determination of suitability. With contempt for law, this sitting judge, with false argument, at every turn attempts to deceive. For example, she claims the determination of suitability is not required prior to appointment in violation of 5 C.F.R. 731.101 (06-5325, p. 9, n 6).

### IRS and Judge McLaughlin above the law

Employees of the IRS, together with Judge McLaughlin, believing themselves above the law, violate law in their self-interest betraying public trust. IRS violating law with impunity is appalling. It shows corrupt IRS employment practice entrenched as normative. Judge McLaughlin accepts the practice and deceptively refuses to review a lawful cause of action, my complaint. The arguments of IRS employees defending their unlawful omission of suitability, and the arguments of Judge McLaughlin defending her nullification of Court jurisdiction, are as sleazy and self-serving a perversion of lawful practice by IRS employees and district court judge as ever came down the pike.

### Equity and the "majesty of the law"

Equity's maxim is, "no wrong without a remedy." Judge McLaughlin's maxim is, no remedy for IRS violation of law by negating the Court's subject matter jurisdiction for review. Judges proclaim their practice as the "majesty of the law," a phrase ringing noble. For Judge McLaughlin, "majesty" is evading review of a lawful cause of action by defending the IRS's unlawful omission of suitability. Defending IRS violations, in order to evade review, is the dark underbelly of the "majesty," as practiced by Judge McLaughlin, decidedly not noble.

### A primer for pro se applicants and attorneys

This case serves as a primer for applicants and attorneys faced with unlawful IRS employment practice, and judicial chicanery.

On advice of the Able Assistant, Judge McLaughlin claims that my litigating as pro se, my "allegations will be held to a less stringent standard <u>Haines v. Kerner</u>, 404 U.S. 519, 520-21 (1972), and must be construed liberally, <u>United States v. Albinson</u>, 356 F.3d 278, 284 n. 9 (3d Cir, 2004." (06-5325, p. 2). Not so, a cynical lie. Judge McLaughlin takes advantage of pro se inexperience to "put one over." For example, she claims "issue preclusion" as ground for dismissal but dismisses for lack of jurisdiction--a deception intended to dupe.

## Exposure, the purpose of this writing

It is in the public interest that it be aware of IRS violations of law, and aware of a judge who protects the IRS in mutual self-interest. Violation of law by the IRS, protected by a judge of the federal district court, is lawless government that undermines the Constitutional protections of the individual from government abuse of power. Lawless government threatens the personal security of the individual.

## IRS, Judge McLaughlin, DOJ defend IRS violations

IRS, Judge McLaughlin, and defense counsel DOJ defend IRS violation of law. The IRS that routinely practices unlawful nonhiring and covers up with deception and outright lies is protected by a federal district court judge who, with her own deception and lies, abets the IRS in order to avoid review of a lawful cause of action, namely, my complaint. Together, they defend the IRS's unlawful nullification of the basic requirement for federal employment, namely, determination of an applicant's suitability for the job for which he applied. Especially egregious is Judge McLaughlin's denying the subject matter jurisdiction assigned her Court by Constitution, statute, and precedent. Capping it off, the DOJ ("J" for justice?) defends the IRS. The IRS, Judge McLaughlin, and the

DOJ three "pillars of the law" cooperate in subverting the law. Bad news for the citizen.

## The corrupt nonhiring practice

First, Director, Personnel Services, Richard J. Cronin, defends Sott's unlawful "failure to act" which is, in fact, the deceptive pretext of a nonexistent application. "Nonexistent" application is, in fact, unlawful <u>concealment</u> of the stated conviction. Concealed conviction underlies the circumvention of suitability. Cronin, complicit with Sott, supports Sott's concealment and perjurious declarations to the Court.

Second, Judge McLaughlin evades review by denying the subject matter jurisdiction of her Court. She claims suitability is not mandated, a negation of 5 C.F.R. 731.101. She claims existence of <u>invisible</u> suitability. She claims issue preclusion as ground for dismissal but, in fact, dismisses on ground of lack of jurisdiction, both fraudulent grounds. She accepts Sott's perjurious <u>declarations</u>. She labels the case "nonprecedential" and fails to publish it, hiding her fraud.

Third, attorneys of the DOJ defend IRS violations. Because the violations cannot be validly defended, they seek to confuse. For example, they create the fallacious term "merits of suitability." "Merits" applies solely to <u>issues</u> of the complaint, that is, IRS violations of employment law. Applied to suitability, "merits" is double-talk obfuscation. What we have is a lying IRS, protected by a deceiving judge, defended by an obfuscating DOJ.

## Deceptive, unlawful nonhiring, standard practice

IRS unlawful omission of suitability is not the work of a single employee or even a few. It is the entire Directorate of Personnel Services that acts in omitting the determination of suitability. The Directorate's employees, able to violate suitability law with impunity, reveal their practice as normative. Judge McLaughlin, evading review, arguing on behalf of the IRS, defends their unlawful practice.

### Judge McLaughlin denies jurisdiction

Two judges in Judge McLaughlin's Court (Judges Giles and Pratter), pursuant to Constitution, statute, Third Cir. (<u>Yeboah v. DOJ</u>), and Supreme Court precedent accept the jurisdiction which Judge McLaughlin denies. She defies Constitution, statute, and precedent and dismisses claiming ground of "issue preclusion," but dismisses on ground of lack of jurisdiction, two phony grounds, a fraudulent dismissal.

### Exposure of IRS and Court malfeasance necessary to public security

Absent "three considerations," IRS employees' claim of "rule of three" as reason for nonhiring is an outright lie, perjury. Judge McLaughlin's claim of "issue preclusion" as ground for dismissal--while she dismisses for lack of jurisdiction--is fraud. Their violations, a raw abuse of governmental power, show contempt for the law and for the public. Violating law with impunity, they demonstrate lawless government.

Protection of the public from those entrusted to implement law--IRS and district court judge--who instead violate law and betray public trust, requires public awareness of their wrongdoing. It is to the benefit of the public to expose their deceptive, lying behavior whenever and wherever it is uncovered. To that end is the purpose of this writing.

www.ingramcontent.com/pod-product-compliance
Lightning Source LLC
Chambersburg PA
CBHW051540170526
45165CB00002B/808